'Christopher Schaefer writes brilliantly with two hands, one for exposing the suffering caused by American militarism, racism, and the neo-conservative Republican economic agenda, and one for exhibiting the compassion, joy, and hope necessary in these difficult times.'

Professor Robert McDermott, California Institute of Integral Studies, President Emeritus.

'By facing the shadow side of our nation, and of himself, Christopher Schaefer makes it possible for us to do the same. *Re-imagining America: Looking for Hope in Difficult Times* is an acorn of hope. May it take root and grow into a mighty oak.'

Eric Utne, founder, Utne Reader.

'By connecting his own journey as an immigrant and a keen student of international politics and economics to the Long Emergency of American Society Christopher Schaefer has done us a real service. These essays bring clarity and hope, connecting our inner soul state to the challenge of creating a more sustainable and just world.'

Paul Mackay, Board chair, Weleda Inc.; former head of the Social Science Section of the School of Spiritual Science at the Goetheanum and until 2018 part of the Executive Board of the General Anthroposophical Society.

'How can we stay informed about world events without suffering from overload? How can we develop empathy for people and events far away? Chris Schaefer's book is a workbook for contemporary humanity. With honesty and wisdom, he shares his insights that will inspire and encourage those who want to make a difference.'

Tom Ravetz, author, *Free from Dogma.*

'In these twelve essays Christopher Schaefer describes the events leading up to the present crises of American democracy. With insight and hope he calls upon us to reflect deeply, reconnect to ourselves and our community and work toward a new tri-sectoral imagination of society which honors our freedom, deepens our democracy and creates a sustainable stake-holder economy.'

Gary Lamb, author, activist and co-director of the Center for Social Research, Hawthorne Valley Association.

To Cyris and Talei, and to Noah and Lela, as well as to all the children of the world.

May the hope, courage and promise of the young help us all to build a society more worthy of the human being.

With Gratitude to

The many people who have read, or heard and commented on, different versions of these essays over the years, and also to those who took the time to read and digest the book, and provide endorsements.

I owe a particular debt of gratitude to Signe Eklund Schaefer whose encouragement, careful reading and many insightful comments have deepened my understanding of the issues discussed and greatly improved the presentation of this book.

While a bit unusual, I would also like to acknowledge the thinkers and authors who have had a significant impact on the development of my thinking in grappling with the perplexing times in which we live.

Hannah Arendt, for her profound insights into the nature of the totalitarian mind.

Alexander Bos, for his reflections on the connection between the human soul and the moral dilemmas of our modern world.

Bernard Lievegoed, for his mentorship and developmental perspectives on human life and the processes of social creation.

Joanna Macy for bringing a sense of agency and hope to thousands of groups and individuals.

Jacob Needleman, for his deep philosophical reflections on the American experience.

Parker Palmer, for his inner honesty and his wisdom in helping people discover the richness of their nature in dialogue with others and with poetry.

Otto Scharmer and Katrin Kaufer for the Presencing work; encouraging people to connect body, soul and spirit in a future-oriented, dynamic process of social transformation.

Rebecca Solnit, for her extraordinary and enlightening essays on the struggle for social equity.

Rudolf Steiner, for his profound spiritual and social insights and for his admonishment to be a conscious witness of our times, which I have tried to take to heart.

And my deep gratitude and appreciation for the millions of people who seek to serve others first, doing the good every day.

RE-IMAGINING AMERICA

FINDING HOPE IN DIFFICULT TIMES

Christopher Schaefer, Ph.D.

Hawthorn Press

Re-Imagining America: Finding Hope in Difficult Times © 2019
Christopher Schaefer Ph.D.

Re-Imagining America: Finding Hope in Difficult Times © 2019 Hawthorn Press, published by Hawthorn Press, Hawthorn House, 1 Lansdown Lane, Stroud, Gloucestershire, GL5 1BJ, UK
info@hawthornpress.com www.hawthornpress.com

Cover Image by Karin Schaefer
Cover design by Lucy Guenot
Typesetting in Minion Pro by Mach 3 Solutions Ltd (www.mach3solutions.co.uk)
Printed by Henry Ling Ltd, The Dorset Press, Dorchester

British Library Cataloguing in Publication Data applied for

ISBN 978-1-907359-96-5

Contents

Foreword

The salvation of the human being is through love and in love.

Viktor Frankl

When I started the *Utne Reader* in 1984, I believed America was on the threshold of a new age. I hoped, and I think we all hoped, that American society would extend human freedom, deepen democracy, and create an economy that served everyone and protected the earth. Instead, we now have a government run by and for the rich, an economy that plunders the earth, and a culture increasingly addicted to entertainment and the internet.

In this, his new book *Re-Imagining America: Finding Hope in Difficult Times*, Christopher Schaefer asks how we got here, and how we can find hope and direction for the future. His first answer is that we clearly witness the times we are living in, and connect key patterns of events. At another level he describes the thought framework lying behind these events, which he refers to as the pattern and ideology of oppression. Behind this ideology he identifies the ultimate causes of our distress. He then points to and describes the great work of re-connection – to nature and the earth, to each other and ourselves – and to the American spirit. He ends by outlining a new covenant between the American people and its government. It is a bracing and ultimately hopeful read.

The theme of war and peace, of conflict and healing, has been a leitmotif in Chris's life, starting with his first memory as a young child during a daylight air-raid in Germany during the Second World War. He studied international politics and practiced conflict resolution and social trans-formation throughout his professional life. He is a global citizen who has seen the world, studied its wisdom traditions and modern thought, and has experienced the challenges and contradictions of our times.

I've known Chris for some 30 years. We first met when he was helping our new City of Lakes Waldorf School in Minneapolis, Minnesota find its legs. Later we served together on the board of Sunbridge Institute, a Waldorf teacher-training college in Spring Valley, New York.

Not long after 9/11, Chris took me on a short drive from the college to High Tor, a hill overlooking the Hudson River. We hiked, climbing through brambles and over barbed wire, then up a steep promontory. From the top of the basalt cliff we could see Manhattan, including the place where the two towers of the World Trade Center had stood. Then Chris told me an old Hudson Valley folk story, the legend of the Ramapo Salamander, that he suggested pointed to the need for re-imagining the American Dream. The story describes a group of miners of European origin who relied on their religious and spiritual traditions as well as their mining experience to safely extract gold, iron ore and gems from the earth. But gradually they became overcome by their lust for wealth and power. Then a giant salamander, a great fire spirit, appeared in the mine, devouring the head miner's wife and son before destroying the mine. Ultimately, through the pure love of the miner's daughter, a symbol of the divine feminine, of Sophia, the fire spirit was restored to its true nature in serving the divine and the progress of humanity.

'Can we also cultivate the true forces of the feminine to help us transform the American Shadow and achieve a new and healthy society?', Chris asked. 'Can we again find the true spirit of America?' This is, indeed, the critical question of our time.

By facing the shadow side of our nation, and of himself, Chris makes it possible for us to do the same. And he does so while maintaining his indomitable sense of hope. In this, Chris reminds me of W.S. Merwin, the great American poet who wrote, 'On the last day of the world, I would want to plant a tree'. *Re-Imagining America: Finding Hope in Difficult Times* is an acorn. May it take root and grow into a mighty oak. It is also a great, good deed, for which I am abundantly grateful.

Eric Utne, founder, *Utne Reader*

Preface

The essays in this volume confirm the author's place as a leader in the still-emerging discipline of *social ecology*. This term was first used in the 1950s by Bernard Lievegoed, Chris Schaefer's inspiring colleague and mentor, as an alternative to 'social pedagogy', in which subject he held a professorial chair at the University of Rotterdam. Social ecology is both science and art: like natural ecology it requires rigorous, objective observation; but also emotional sensitivity and a commitment to action. Throughout his career as academic, researcher, consultant and social practitioner Chris has exemplified and deepened this approach, working with groups and organisations to develop innovative initiatives, bring vision into action and learn from the experience of implementing change.

Just as natural ecology integrates an understanding of the nature, development and behaviour of individual organisms with an appreciation of their systemic interdependence – with each other and their environmental context – so a valid social ecology must include both profound insight into the visceral and psychic realities of individual human beings, and the identification and characterisation of their interrelationships on micro-, meso- and macro-social levels. Without the former, we would lose ourselves in abstract socio-economic theory; without the latter, we would be trapped in the Thatcherite illusion that 'there is no such thing as society'.

Human beings create social forms in their own image. Because of this, human self-understanding is critical to social development, and a full, balanced picture of what it means to be human is essential to the health of organisations and societies. As Chris describes, social-ecological research starts with immersing oneself in perceptible *phenomena*, allowing them to work in us through contemplation and compassion, recognising also in ourselves the social and anti-social forces that give rise to justice and injustice, prejudice and acceptance, exclusion and inclusion in society.

Through this 'witnessing' of events, trends and turning points, we may move to a perception of the phenomena as *symptoms* of social sickness and health, of significant developments and challenges to which we can respond in ways which are more balanced and free than our often impulsive reactions.

Particularly striking about this book of essays, written over years of careful political and social observation, are the connections established between political, economic, psychological and foreign policy issues. The arguments linking 9/11, the 'War on Terror', the Economic Crisis and the election of Donald Trump as manifestations of an effort to undermine the American Spirit and corrupt the American Soul are particularly thought-provoking and morally challenging for a society prone to short memory and an easy acceptance of government-sanctioned versions of the truth.

Such heightened insight and deepened perception, however, is only the first step on the path towards social healing which all the chapters in this book invite us to follow. In multiple contexts, from many different perspectives, the author leads us from insight to empathy to intervention, opening our hearts as well as our minds and stimulating us to whatever transformative action our life-situation enables us to take. Along the way he introduces us to a community of fellow-travellers – thinkers, activists and artists who can be our companions, as they have been his, on this most important of journeys.

In the last three essays, Chris brings his diagnosis right up to the present Difficult Times, with penetrating analyses not only of the delusional thinking behind the current forces working in American society, but also how those forces, which oppose and distort healthy social relationships, can be found at work in our own souls. The final essay is an idealistic *tour de force*, in which he paints an inspiring, detailed and specific image of actions that could and should be taken to save the US from its own shadow.

For British readers there is much of relevance here; much to be learned not only about our most powerful 'ally' but also about the forces of fragmentation and discord which are also at work here. As the tragi-comic, slow-motion train crash of Brexit is in danger of driving a confused, divided UK into the ecocidal arms of Trump and the Saudi weapons buyers, we need to take note of the insights and healing impulses which this book offers.

Steve Briault, Director of Development,
Emerson College, Sussex

Introduction

> The task of the mind is to understand what happened and this under-
> standing, according to Hegel, is man's way of reconciling himself with
> reality; its actual end is to be at peace with the world.
>
> Hannah Arendt

As a young person studying international politics and economics, I ran
across a slim volume by Hannah Arendt called *Between Past and Future:
Six Exercises in Political Thought*, which I have carried with me for many
years and through many moves.[1] What appealed to me in her work was
the combination of philosophical reflection and historical insight. In
her preface, Arendt articulates two longings which I share: the desire to
understand the past sufficiently well that the main outlines of the future
become visible; and secondly, to connect the realm of theory, of ideas, to
the realm of praxis, of social action, in a tangible and authentic manner.

She cites De Tocqueville's lament, when, after having completed his
justly celebrated *Democracy in America*, he noted, 'Since the past has
ceased to throw its light upon the future the mind of man wanders in
obscurity'.[2] Do we not share this lament when looking at the perplexities
of the present moment in American history, and scratch our heads and
wonder how we got here, with a deadlocked Congress and an unhinged
President?

Certainly, the desire to understand the patterns of history, to see
elements of the present and future encapsulated in events of the past,
has been with me from the time of my undergraduate study of philosophy and history, and later graduate work in international politics
and economics. The search for underlying structures of meaning, for
having a lens through which to connect past and future, led me on a
long and still ongoing search through critical theory, neo-Marxism,
social phenomenology and the philosophy of social science. In this

search, the evolution of consciousness in human history, as articulated by writers and thinkers such as Edmund Husserl, Owen Barfield, Teilhard de Chardin, P.A. Sorokin, Rudolf Steiner and Richard Tarnas, spoke to me.[3] Within the flow of history and the evolution of cultures, I sensed a shift of human awareness from a greater embeddedness in nature and community and a reliance on tradition – what Barfield calls 'original participation' – to the more isolated, self-centred, materialistic and individualized consciousness of the modern era. This perspective informs many of the essays collected in this book, and has led me to follow issues over time, and to connect problems in American economic and social life to the type of consciousness underlying the social structures, processes and behaviors described.

My search for meaning in history as a young person was also linked to the search for meaning in my own life, and led me to explore questions of inner development, biographical themes and, ultimately, to considerations of reincarnation and karma as a way of understanding my life.

The relationship between the realm of theory, of ideas and the sense world of actions and practice is the second tension to which Arendt refers. This tension between the real and the ideal is acute for anyone genuinely concerned about questions of social justice and social reform because it touches on questions of personal authenticity, and of course on social-change strategy. In getting older I increasingly experience that unless I attempt to understand and practice the values I espouse, with all of the difficulties that this entails, I lack the moral foundation for promoting greater justice and equality in society. Gandhi, Martin Luther King, Nelson Mandela, Rosa Parks and Rigoberta Menchu are individuals whose social and political leadership rested on a strong personal moral foundation. Donald Trump, and many other politicians and world leaders today, make visible what happens when there is a decoupling of individual morality from the exercise of influence and power.

The essays in this volume also have their source in the repeated reminder of the profound human suffering caused by war, conflict, hatred and prejudice built into the experiences of my life. My first memory as a three-year old was a daylight air raid on Frankfurt in early 1945, the sky dark with planes and the ground trembling from their roar as they passed overhead. Then there was the experience of playing in bomb craters and destroyed tanks in the fields and forests surrounding my home, and witnessing the returning veterans of war, often maimed in body and soul.

Not much later, as a seven-year old immigrant, I remember standing on the deck of a US troop transport steaming into New York harbor with the sun setting behind the Statue of Liberty, being excited about the prospect of a new life but full of apprehension about what we would meet. As it was 1950, it was not surprising to experience prejudice in our first days at school when signs of 'Nazi go home' appeared on my desk, and my siblings and I learned to defend ourselves against playground bullies. But this was a temporary set-back, vanishing as our English improved, and because we were white.

After my sophomore year in college, I spent six months in Berlin at the Free University, arriving a week after the Wall went up, in August of 1961. As I had an American passport and spoke German well, I was able to pass into the Russian sector of what was to become East Berlin. I remember being at Check Point Charlie and seeing American and British Forces, troops and tanks, lined up on one side of barbed wire barricades, and Russian tanks, artillery and troops on the other. As I became involved in smuggling my aunt and others out of East Germany, I also learned that what moved most people to leave their home was the prospect of better jobs, refrigerators and television sets, and less dreams about freedom and democracy, as I had believed in my youthful naïveté.

While visiting and talking to people in East Berlin I also met a deeply religious group of young people who decided to stay and witness what was happening to their society under Communism. For the most part they were members of the Confessing Church, a part of the Lutheran Church started by Dietrich Bonhoeffer and active in the resistance movement against Hitler and the Nazis. This group was later to play a significant role in the overthrow of Communism in 1989.

After returning to finish college I was shocked by the Kennedy assassination in 1963, as were most Americans. At the same time, I was majoring in European History with a focus on understanding Nazism and the German Resistance Movement. This study of Hitler and the Nazis had a profound impact on me. First, it awoke me to the dangers of official government accounts, and the press manipulating public opinion and often hiding true motives and the underlying truth. Secondly, it enabled me to appreciate the dangers of nationalism, of racism, and of the horrors of genocide against the Jews, and indeed against all minorities. It also made me aware of what a thin veneer civilization really is, how many Germans actively participated in the extreme cruelty, horror, and sadism of the concentration camps, and how such perversions of human decency can find a home within most human beings, given the right circumstances. Lastly, in studying the resistance to Hitler, including the White Rose Movement and the Kreisau Circle, I realized what great courage it took to witness and combat evil, and how whole families, such as the Bonhoeffers, or the Scholl siblings, gave their lives in acts of resistance.

I was finishing my graduate work and was in Washington D.C. when Martin Luther King and Robert Kennedy were assassinated, and I experienced the race riots in downtown D.C. This was another awakening to issues of prejudice and injustice, followed by my growing involvement in the anti-Vietnam war movement. Having studied International Politics and American Foreign Policy, I knew that the Chinese and the Vietnamese had a long history of enmity and conflict, making a lie of the domino theory. So I demonstrated and spoke out against the war, as millions of others did. One of life's ironies was participating in demonstrations against my own department at the Massachusetts Institute of Technology, where I had begun teaching international politics and American foreign policy in 1969, for its role in developing the strategic hamlet program in Vietnam.

Life, family and work as a consultant and advisor to communities and organizations, and as a teacher and adult educator, consumed most of my time and consciousness in the ensuing years. It was during these years of the 1980s and 1990s that I worked on questions of conflict and human development, discovering the difficulties of peace-building in communities, and in myself. It was during those years that I also discovered the importance of conversation, of meeting, of group work and of building a family and a marriage; learnings and insights which provided the basis for the essay on the work of re-connection toward the end of this book.

The next great awakening for me was 9/11, which shook me to my roots, and fully awoke me to the American Empire Project and its attendant tragedies: the wars in Afghanistan and Iraq, the global economic crisis, and what I increasingly think of as the time of the Long Emergency, with its portends of ecological disaster.

This description of my biographical journey in relation to the events of our time, while far from unique for someone coming of age in the 1960s, is the personal foundation for the essays in this book. The essays are my effort to understand the times we live in, with a particular focus on the corruption and decline of the United States as a once great nation. Or to put this another way, they are an anguished cry of disillusionment from an older, Ivy League-educated white male, who was socialized to be part of the system, and who only woke up fully to its internal contradictions and grave moral lapses after 9/11.

I think we write to make sense of our life and thoughts, and in so doing we hope that our questions and insights will be of interest to others. That is certainly true of these essays, which are a record in time of my attempt to be a witness to our times, of trying to understand the often inexplicable nature of political and social events since 2001.

The essays cover the time period from 1989, the fall of the Soviet Union and of the Communist bloc in Eastern Europe, to the present day. They are reflections and commentaries on the times: either essays, talks or seminars, given or published between 2004 and the spring of 2019. Except for minor editing, and in a few instances, some updating, they were not changed from the time of publication or presentation. They are a sequential commentary on the times, and did not form an interconnected whole in my mind until the election of Donald Trump to the presidency of the United States. Then I could see that the betrayal of our core values through the pursuit of the American Empire Project, with its attendant undermining of our economic and political system, called forth this perfect symbol of the American shadow – of our unredeemed self – in a vain, narcissistic, racist, lying, power-hungry, insecure and misogynistic businessman.

We have come home and occupied ourselves, and are now living in what I consider to be the fourth great period of crisis and transition in American history. The first was during the time of our founding, the Revolutionary Period, 1770–86, the second during the Civil War, 1850–66, the third from the Great Depression through the end of World War II, 1928–46, and the fourth, from 2001 to the present day. It seems that about every 80 years, American society meets fundamental challenges which threaten its future as a democracy. We again face the question of what kind of a society we will be, and whether or not we will be able as a people to extend human freedom, democracy, and economic justice, and whether we will choose the ideology of oppression, of injustice, domination and therefore decline.

The essays cover diverse yet interconnected themes; what it means to be a conscious witness of our times, questions about 9/11, the second Bush administration and the American empire project, the global economic crisis, income inequalities, navigating chaos and the election of Donald Trump, as well as ideas about social reform and our common future. They are written in differing styles, some more reflective and personal, some more scholarly, and some expressing outrage, mirroring the different contexts in which they were offered.

When read in sequence, they offer one account of how American economic and political elites have undermined democracy and drastically weakened our nation, while causing untold suffering in the Middle East and around the world. They also point in the direction of what we can do, individually and together to restore America as 'the fact, the symbol and the promise of a new beginning', and of how we may make a lasting difference in our communities and in our times.[4]

Christopher Schaefer
Great Barrington, Mass.
2 December 2018

Notes

1   Hannah Arendt, *Between Past and Future: Six Exercises in Political Thought*, The World Publishing Company, New York, 1963. Quotation from page 8.
2   Quoted in Arendt, p. 7.
3   E. Husserl, *Ideas: General Introduction to Pure Phenomenology*, Collier Books, New York, 1962, pp. 100–133; Owen Barfield, *Saving the Appearances: A Study of Idolatry*, Wesleyan University Press, Middletown, Conn., 1965 ; P.A Sorokin, *The Crisis of Our Age: The Social and Cultural Outlook*, E.P. Dutton and Co, New York, 1941; R. Steiner, 'Social and Anti-Social in the Human Being', 1918, Rudolf Steiner Archive, at www.rsarchive.com; R. Tarnas, *The Passion of the Western Mind: Understanding the Ideas That Have Shaped Our World View*, Harmony Books, New York, 1992.
4   Jacob Needleman, *The American Soul: Rediscovering the Wisdom of the Founders*, Tarcher/Putnam, New York, 2002, p. 5.

Part I:

Being a Witness of Our Times

Chapter 1

Witnessing the Long Emergency
(*August 2017*)

Not everything that is faced can be changed, but nothing can be changed
until it is faced.

James Baldwin

Each day we are bombarded with fear-producing events vying for our
attention and our sympathy. The melting of glaciers and global sea rise,
the plight of three million Syrian refugees in Turkish camps, the growing
levels of starvation in Central Africa and the growth of xenophobia in the
United States and many European countries assault us. I wish, and I think
we all wish, for a return to a sense of normalcy; the flow and pattern of
the seasons, the playing of children on the playground waiting for the ice
cream truck on a warm summer afternoon, holidays and family events,
and of course for leaders whom we can trust and institutions that embody
a sense of morality. Instead, given the fragility of the environment and
of society as well as the omnipresent global media, we are assured of
being confronted with human suffering, perceived existential threats, and
immoral and cruel acts by individuals and governments.

We are living in the age of what I call 'The Long Emergency', to borrow
the title of James Kunstler's book, and need to become conscious, both
about how we relate to the media and how we can develop an inner
and outer practice of witnessing what is happening in the world and in
ourselves.[1] Without such a practice I fear we lose our balance and become
more anxious, fearful and easily manipulated individuals.

The Long Emergency

For me 9/11 was the beginning of what I think of as the Long Emergency, when the break-down of the post-Second World War order became visible, and when many of the taken-for-granted assumptions about private and public life no longer held true in the United States and in many parts of the world. Members of Al Qaeda, mostly Saudi citizens, were described as having flown two jet liners into the Twin Towers in New York and supposedly also one into the Pentagon. I spent days glued to the television asking is this really possible and wondering about the circumstances which allowed inexperienced pilots to fly sophisticated aircraft through densely patrolled airspace into downtown Manhattan without being intercepted.

What followed was the War on Terror, the Patriot Act and vastly increased domestic and international surveillance. The USA invaded Afghanistan and a few years later Iraq, despite no credible evidence of any linkage between Al Qaeda and Saddam Hussein or of weapons of mass destruction in Iraq. The war in Afghanistan is ongoing, now entering its 16th year, and we are still engaged in Iraq and in Syria, fighting a newly emerging form of Islamic terrorism, Islamic State or ISIL. Instability in the Middle East, Africa, Ukraine and Afghanistan continues with Western efforts at regime change adding to the flood of refugees seeking safety. Suicide bombers now threaten most countries of Europe, and North America as well as many parts of Asia, giving rise to new forms of nationalism and authoritarianism while undermining the postwar consensus on the value of the EU, the importance of the international political order, and the nature of freedom in democratic societies.

At the same time the global threat of climate change increases, with mass species extinctions, rising sea levels, dramatic weather shifts and unheard-of levels of pollution in China, India Pakistan and the urban areas of central and South America. Drought has wrought havoc in Africa and elsewhere with 40–60 million people facing food insecurity and starvation. Deeply moving pictures of starving people looking for food and water on a parched landscape proliferate while the United Nations is unable to fund its multiple requests for humanitarian aid.

The pattern of disturbing events continued with the global financial crisis of 2008–10 requiring a massive government bail-out in the United States while it wiped out 40 per cent of the collective wealth of ordinary Americans, many of them inner city residents. At the same time globalization and computerization hollowed out the industries of the Mid West and helped to generate the greatest wealth inequalities in the United States since the Great Depression. The recent Brexit vote in Great Britain and the election of the manifestly unfit Donald Trump to the Presidency of the United States rounds off this brief summary of why we have entered uncharted waters in understanding the dynamics of the times we live in. We appear to be adrift, awaiting the inexplicable, and not knowing what to expect or do.

As I paint a largely negative and in many ways depressing picture of our present situation in the following essays I would like to note that my focus is largely on economic and political developments in the United States and that I fully recognize that in many respects there has been significant progress globally in regard to disease and infant mortality, education and literacy, and violence and war. The increase in world population is slowing down, some animal species have been saved from extinction and women's right are improving in many parts of the world. Poverty, crime and even drug use is also declining in the United States, despite the opioid epidemic. So I am not unaware of the real objective progress that has been achieved in the world over the last decades, in particular in Asia and Africa. I agree with Hans Rosling, the Swedish health statistician, that the right attitude to cultivate toward the state of the world is that it is both bad and better at the same time. And I add as Joshua Rothman noted: 'the spirit of progress is also the spirit of discontent'.[2]

Yet it is worth asking why my pessimistic assessment of the present and the future is shared by so many people in the United States and in many other countries.[3] Certainly, the global and visceral nature of the news promoting crises and fear plays a role. The visible corruption of our business and political elites in the United States and elsewhere is also a factor. Remember the Panama papers in 2016, and the Paradise papers in 2017, showing how global political and economic elites and corporations, including the Queen of England, some of Trump's cabinet, and companies such as Apple, Walmart, Facebook, Nike, and Siemens, have moved their assets overseas to avoid taxes while the majority of Americans have experienced flat wages, limited savings, and declining prospects.

When we cannot trust the institutions of society to do their job properly, and when politicians are bought and sold by unlimited amounts of dark money, with the average price of a Senate campaign estimated to be $19 million, it is easy to lose trust. If you add the visible and growing crisis of climate change to the realization that American society does not provide a real safety net, adequate healthcare or equitable access to affordable and quality higher education, never mind a secure retirement, we appear to be on our own. This is truly a daunting prospect for the 50 per cent of Americans who have difficulty meeting an unexpected emergency bill of $500 or the 30 per cent of the elderly with no retirement savings except for Social Security.[4] The question of who stole the American Dream is therefore an important question, and the answer is not immigrants, Muslims, Mexicans or liberals but rather the ideas, values and behavior of the kleptocracy of political and economic elites so evident in the cabinet of the present Trump administration, in the halls of Congress and in the boardrooms of corporations.

To find a balance to the daily dose of depressing political and social news, we need to look for the many positives happening outside the formal structures of power, the free medical clinic staffed by dentists, doctors and nurses in my local community, or the peaceful Women's March following the Trump inauguration. Indeed, to see and experience the positive, caring and healing dimensions of public and private life becomes an essential part of a conscious practice of witnessing our times. To marvel at a young child's infectious smile, to be grateful for a deep conversation with a good friend, are small but important antidotes to the grimmer aspects of modern reality.

As I spend a good bit of time in my garden, I also want to point to the healing possibilities of nature, described so beautifully by Mary Oliver in her poem 'Late Spring':

> …Finally the world is beginning
> To change, its fevers mounting,
> Its leaves unfolding.
> And the mockingbirds find
> Ample reason and breath to fashion
> New songs. They do. You can
> Count on it….[5]

Given the bewildering state of the world and the manipulative, aggressive and sometimes false nature of the media, we also need to become conscious of what, when and with what frequency we attend to the news and to then monitor our reactions. When I do this, I notice a clear tension between engagement, between involvement, and withdrawal.

Withdrawal or Engagement?

One reaction to the threatening nature of our times is that of disengagement, of distancing, of not wanting to let an event or an aspect of human suffering into my consciousness. I might say I will think about the families threatened by deportation to Mexico later, or I cannot really deal with the frequent drownings of North Africans crossing the Mediterranean now. I avoid taking in the situation, largely because I feel powerless to do anything about it. So instead, I go out to garden, read a book or visit with friends. The process of withdrawal may go further still, with people deciding to protect themselves and their families from a corrupt and dangerous world by moving to a rural area or to New Zealand. Ultimately the tendency toward withdrawal leads to isolation, to depression and in some cases, to mental illness. The Unabomber, Ted Kaczynski, is an extreme example of this, as he withdrew from society in moving to rural Montana in the 1980s, and then began mailing bombs to selected individuals over a 20-year period. In his case, withdrawal and violence were combined, bringing the contradictory reactions to an alienating world into a deeper connection.

A second basic response is engagement; we donate money, we petition, we join political and environmental groups. This is often helpful; volunteering for important work, giving of our time and our heart. Yet intense engagement can also have its dangers, leading to frenetic activity, burnout and to such deep emotional attachment that our life and consciousness become consumed. The response to the election of Trump and the active resistance that individuals engage in can become an obsession, as can opposition to the racism, fascism and misogyny still present in our society. It is not so surprising that deep emotional engagement can also lead to violence and terrorism.

I do find the psychic impact of war, of rape and of extreme violence or of genocide in Rwanda, Syria, Bosnia or Myanmar extremely difficult to contemplate and to allow into my soul. With such instances of our inhumanity toward each other I think that Elizabeth Kubler-Ross's description of responses to the knowledge of imminent death in her classic study *On Death and Dying* can be deeply illuminating. She lists five responses, beginning with *denial* – is this really happening or was it a dream?; moving to *anger*, an emotional response to powerlessness, betrayal or physical hurt, and then to *bargaining* – will the threat of serious illness, or public shaming or terrorism be lifted if I pray to God, become a more moral and generous person or choose some other act of sacrifice or transformation?

I can find these emotional reactions in myself and with my friends and colleagues when I remember our responses to Kennedy's assassination in 1963, to 9/11, and even to Trump's election, as well as to more private tragic events. The fourth response, that of *depression*, is also possible to locate in oneself when one considers how people react to trauma, followed over time by *acceptance* – the Brexit vote happened, and Trump is now the President of the United States.[6]

There are, of course, a great variety of responses to news and to world events, including that of a psychic fix, the jolt of Schadenfreude toward the suffering of others. What I think is important is that we learn to observe these reactions in ourselves and to monitor and, if need be, to modify our responses when they lead to obsession, to contemplating violence or to depression or other inner disturbances. In the end I believe that by attending to our inner responses to the events of our world we gain in both self-knowledge and world knowledge, and we become a witness of our age.

Why Be a Witness?

In observing the difficult times in which we live, it is tempting to say – 'Why bother? – why let the suffering of the other, of the displaced, the victims of war or terrorism or of the sick and the poor into our consciousness?'.

I describe some of my reasons for engaging with and witnessing our times and ask you to note your own reflections:

1   By being aware of what is happening in the world around me I begin the journey of overcoming my feelings of powerlessness and alienation. Observing, taking in, is often followed by a call to understanding and in many cases to activity. Kinder Morgan, an energy company, is building a pipeline through the Otis State Forest near my hometown which most studies show is not needed for local or regional energy consumption. By paying attention I become aware of this fact and can act by petition, vote or demonstration. The threat to deport illegal immigrants pronounced by the Trump administration affects the Latino population of Berkshire County where I live and people whom I know and care about. Recently in a town meeting we passed a resolution supporting immigrants, minorities and people of all faiths and orientations, in order to create a safer, more inclusive and caring community.

Without being aware of events I would have missed the meeting and not been able to vote my conscience.

2   Since we as human beings create the social world of conversations, relationships, towns, roads, governments and nations then surely I have an obligation to understand our society as best as I can and to be an active participant in its formation. Without interest, understanding and engagement in the social world by large numbers of people, a functioning democracy is not possible.

3   In a letter from a Birmingham, Alabama jail, Martin Luther King wrote to his fellow clergy about the scourge of racism:

> All men are caught in an inescapable network of mutuality, tied in a single garment of destiny. Whatever affects one directly, affects all indirectly. I can never be what I ought to be, until you are what you ought to be and you can never be what you ought to be until I am what I ought to be....[7]

Our mind and, indeed, modern consciousness may suggest that we are separate, autonomous beings, but any reflection about the nature of society and our relation to others leads to recognizing that racism and prejudice, or the fact that millions of children go to bed hungry around the world every night, also affects me, sometimes directly and, most often, indirectly.

One of the advantages of the modern media is that it can bring to our consciousness what slumbers in our sub-consciousness; the struggles and achievements of our brothers and sisters in other communities around the world. I have begun an inner and an outer picture gallery to remind me; a mother in Africa looking for water for her children at dawn, a family huddling for safety in Mosul, the scarred back of a day laborer in India or the joyful smile of a new mother in Detroit.

This gallery of images helps me to escape the narrow fetters of my own concerns and enhances my gratitude for life. I can never be who I am meant to be without developing more compassion and love, and you can never be who you ought to be if you are suffering discrimination, hunger, violence and fear, as Martin Luther King wrote so eloquently many years ago. It really is a question of trying to make the concerns of the other your own, as the second great commandment of the New Testament asks us to do, 'Love Your

Neighbor as Yourself'.[8] This moral injunction is expressed in all of the world's great religions; thus, Hillel, the great Jewish teacher, says to a student seeking his advice, 'That which is despicable to you, do not do unto others. This is the whole Torah and the rest is commentary.'

4   There is also a clear moral and ethical dimension to understanding and witnessing the world we are part of. I do not mean that in a narrow pre-defined religious sense. But if we recall the profound evil which Hitler, Mao and Stalin unleashed on their citizens and the world in the twentieth century through the imprisonment and killing of millions of people, and we think of the genocide in Germany, Bosnia and Rwanda and the rape, slavery, and wanton killings now used as weapons of war in Africa and the Middle East, we must shudder and acknowledge the faces and gestures of evil. Closer to home, what do we do with prejudice against immigrants, racism against Latinos and Africans, and misogyny against women, or with expressions of our own anger or cruelty toward a child, a partner or a friend?

I would define evil as actions, policies, goals and activities which suppress human freedom and equality, which limit diversity, and which create structures and patterns of exploitation in which the few dominate the many for their own interests. If I apply this perspective more broadly, then saddling students with mountains of debt for their college education or deporting parents of children because they are here illegally or closing down health clinics for women and the poor is evil and, in my view, profoundly un-Christian. I think that evil is strongly connected to egotism and fear, and in its institutional forms seeks to downgrade the human being, to make life a struggle for survival. It ultimately stems from isolation from others and the world, a separation from nature, from love, from community, and it seeks domination over all that is not self.

Goodness, on the other hand, rests on a felt sense of connection to the world, to the natural, human and divine community of which we are part. We have all experienced people, regardless of their station in life, who embrace life, diversity, human freedom and equality and seek 'beloved community' with others. After the killing of nine African Americans in a church in Charleston, South Carolina in 2015, a black State Trooper, at a rally protesting the removal of the Confederate flag, was photographed gently guiding an elderly white supremacist to a seat in the heat. The photo went viral and when Leroy Smith, the trooper, was asked about the reason for his act, he said, 'Love'.[9]

There are many, many people in our communities and around the world committed to giving, to selflessness and to love; they do the good every day. Make a list for yourself of the people in your town, community of friends or network of acquaintances who manifest these moral qualities. If you need inspiration look at Nicholas Kristof and Sheryl WuDunn's book, *A Path Appears: Transforming Lives, Creating Opportunity*, or Sarah van Gelder's *The Revolution where You Live*.[10]

By witnessing the ethical and moral struggle between the qualities of good and evil in the world, we awaken to that struggle in ourselves. The decisive recognition is that we are each capable of evil, that the struggle between the progressive forces of life, freedom, diversity and creativity and its opposites takes place in our soul every day as well as in the world. This recognition, when kept in consciousness, limits fundamentalism, enhances modesty and increases humility. It stops us from demonizing the other because we are willing to face the darkness in our own soul, and it encourages us to both engage with the world and to work on our own transformation.

In witnessing our times I believe it is essential to go on both an inner and an outer journey. The inner journey needs to contain those essential elements found in all true spiritual traditions, the practice of reverence and gratitude as a foundation for inner work, mindfulness exercises and meditation and prayer. It is only when we have some mastery over our soul, such as can be achieved through working on Rudolf Steiner's six exercises or in a very different way with the eightfold path of Buddha, that our thinking, feeling and willing is capable of becoming an instrument of perception. Then we become more able to witness and to transform what is happening in our time, through what I call a path of insight, a journey of compassion, and the practice of a healing will.

The Path of Insight

Through the schooling of our thinking life we develop the capacity to direct our attention to perceiving and understanding what is happening around us in the world. This implies not only being aware of issues in the moment such as the recent withdrawal of the United States from the Paris Climate Accords by the Trump administration, but also to developing an understanding of issue linkages, of how different events are connected over time. What, for example, is the connection between the Trump election and the wars in the Middle East – wars which were started by the administration of George W. Bush, and continued in a more muted fashion by Barack Obama? One very obvious one is that over $5 trillion has been spent on our military adventures in Afghanistan and Iraq. This is money that could have been spent on infrastructure, on education, and on re-imagining the economic basis of life in the industrial heartland of America. It could have been used to fund a single payer health system and to deal with the great inequality of wealth in America. 'No Middle Eastern wars, no Donald Trump' is a quick summary.

Our wars in the Middle East are also one of the main causes of ISIL, the Taliban and radical Islam in general, for in the eyes of many Muslims we are the New Crusaders, echoing the invasions of the Middle East by the European knights of the eleventh, twelfth and thirteenth centuries. And it is not just our armies that are perceived as a threat, but our secular, materialistic values and life style spread through the ubiquitous world wide web. It really is a case of Jihad vs. McWorld, which, while appearing to be opposites, are both threats to democracy, as Benjamin Barber argues.[11]

The path of understanding made possible by focusing our thinking on issues of concern involves not only developing interest and finding linkages between issues but also in looking behind phenomena for the underlying systems, values and ideas which created and animated this world we are seeking to understand and transform. I think that John Maynard Keynes, the famous British economist, was quite right when he suggested that it is economic and social ideas which determine the kind of society we create. He noted 'soon or late it is ideas, not vested interests, which are dangerous for good or evil'.[12]

By way of illustration, in April 2017 American Airlines agreed to a new contract with its pilots and other employees, raising wages. But the financial industry complained, with Jaime Baker of JPMorgan stating, 'We are troubled by AAL's wealth transfer of nearly 1 billion to its labor groups'.[13] Such a public statement is a deed, just as the new labor contract is. They take place in the context of a capitalistic system in the United States in which the power and size of the financial industry has dramatically increased in the last decades despite that industry's central role in causing the global economic crisis of 2007–9.

The values of this capitalist system include competition between companies, the virtues of markets in establishing price and in allocating resources intelligently (land, labor and capital), and limiting the power and size of government. They include promoting free trade and ensuring a legal system that protects the interests of capital and private owner-ship. Central as well to the values of this Neo-Liberal Economic Canon, embraced by the Republican party since the time of Ronald Reagan and Margaret Thatcher, is the idea that management has a primary legal responsibility to shareholders, so that paying reasonable wages or taking responsibility for environmental damage caused by a company is not only misguided but also possibly illegal. These ideas promote a world of competition in which the community, workers and the less fortunate are ignored. It is cut-throat capitalism in which the struggle for survival is the dominant ideology.

Developing a deeper interest in the social, political and economic world and attempting to understand the issues which limit our freedom, crea-tivity and responsibility is an ongoing task. I think of it as uncovering the signature of oppression, of deciphering the many ways in which indi-viduals, groups and governments undermine the freedom, creativity and well-being of minority groups and individuals and indeed of us all. As Justice William Douglass of the US Supreme Court warned many years ago:

> As nightfall does not come at once, neither does oppression. In both instances, there is a twilight when everything remains seemingly unchanged. And it is in such twilight that we must all be most aware of change in the air – however slight – lest we become unwitting victims of the darkness.[14]

Developing Empathy: The Journey of Compassion

Attempting to understand the social world requires us to pay attention and to manifest sustained interest in following issues over time. It also asks us to look behind the phenomena in order to understand the prin-ciples and formative ideas which lie behind the systems and behavior of the social world. While this path requires engagement and discipline it does allow us to keep events at a distance, at arm's length, avoiding the pain and the feelings of powerlessness which the world inflicts on so many people. However, this potential one-sidedness can be balanced by adding another dimension to the task of witnessing our times, practicing the path of empathy, of deep compassion.

This, again, is best practiced in moments of inner quiet when I can, for example, take in the recent attacks at London Bridge, or the conflict in Mosul, or the prejudice experienced by a young African American student at our local High School. Of course, there are limits to the number of situations we can take in at any one time, but it is surprising to note that if we create moments of quiet each day and begin to listen deeply, situations will begin to speak to us. For me this often starts with pictures or images, which is why I mentioned earlier the inner and outer picture gallery which I create for myself. But once these images begin to move, to speak, then I begin to experience empathy, often for both the victim and the perpetrator.

Empathy does not mean sympathy or criticism. It means a taking in of the other's experience, best captured by the German word 'Mitleid', a co-suffering with the other. Last winter I was attempting to live into the experiences of a group of Syrian refugees blocked at the Hungarian border in a snow storm and also, some days later, that of a young ISIL fighter holed up in an apartment block in Mosul. In each of these situations I found that after some time the individuals and their feelings, their hopes and their despair began to come alive in me. I would revisit these situations a number of times in the following days and found a deep compassion arise, while also recognizing the unacceptable nature of these situations.

Christine Gruwez, in her essays on *Walking with Your Time*, describes this as a step of inwardness, of deep listening and of creating a resonating chamber in our heart. She adds:

> In other words, we let the events that are acted out on the world stage deeply within us, so deeply that it might be said that we make them part of our own being…. I no longer want to just study what has happened, to consider it and look into it – I aim to allow it to be and to absorb it into myself…[15]

Gruwez then describes a third step, that of accepting and receiving. She sees this as accepting the signature of evil in our time, of the egotism and the separation from others and the world. If we can do this, and it requires ongoing practice, then we experience a feeling of profound compassion and this in turn allows a force to come into our soul, a new ability to carry the burdens of our age. It is not a solution, nor a prescription of what must be done, but a willingness to carry, to witness. This, Gruwez suggests, then becomes a fourth step, to work out of a new presence of mind and heart. I experience it as having a source which is not our ordinary consciousness but rather a new, wiser source of guidance. Now, in moments, we are able to be in touch with the healing power of the spirit of humanity.

We can have such an experience when out of deep listening to another person or group we are moved to say something or to act in a far wiser way than normal, and we have a feeling that the other's deep longing has spoken through us. We can also have such an experience in conversation with the world when we let world events resonate deeply within us and integrate them into our soul. For me the refugees in Hungary, the scared ISIL fighter and a young African American in Mississippi suffering from AIDS without adequate medical or counseling support are alive, they resonate in my being. And when I carry these people and their situations in myself a deep feeling of compassion arises that is met by a calm holding strength. It is as if my effort to open my heart is beheld, strengthened and supported by another spiritual force which meets me.

I experience doing such work as a kind of breathing, breathing in the world, breathing out compassion. It can also be practiced in a short form, which I attempt after having lived inwardly with a situation for 10–15 minutes, a practice called Tonglen by Buddhists. Breathe in the suffering and the struggle of the other in image form and breathe out compassion and love. Carrying out such a practice over time leads to sensing a force of healing, of positivity filling your soul and giving a blessing to life despite all of its hardships.[16]

Transformation: Practicing a Healing Will

There are many ways in which we engage with the world to bring healing and transformation. We join groups devoted to environmental preservation, social justice, women and minority rights; we demonstrate, petition and vote, and we support a myriad of important causes with donations and time. In being active we become part of the 'Blessed Unrest', the millions of people around the world seeking to create a better world for our children and grand-children. We are then part of civil society which seeks to balance and to block the often unhealthy alliance between big business and big government.

In addition, many of us, seeing a need, have started initiatives seeking a better way forward. Judy Wicks founded the White Dog Café in 1983, outside of Philadelphia, and developed a local food-based economy. She then went on to co-found BALLE, the Business Alliance for Local Living Economies. Or a friend, Bea Birch, who for years wanted to see an alternative to drug-based forms of treating the mentally ill, and unable to get hospitals interested, started Inner Fire, a new therapy center in Vermont. Another example is the young violin soloist in Boston who last year gave or arranged for 60 concerts of high quality to be held in homeless shelters in the Boston area. If we look around us and reflect on our own lives we will discover a myriad of initiatives, of new activities we and others are busy with, all attempting to create a more caring world.

By pointing to these individual acts of courage and initiative I do not want to minimize the great impact of the larger movements for social change which have transformed our lives for the better in the twentieth and twenty-first centuries; the women's movement, the civil rights movement, the environmental movement, the organic agriculture movement and many others. But these too were started by individuals who somehow captured the spirit of the times and moved others to join them; for example, Rosa Parks and Martin Luther King, or Rachel Carson and her book, *Silent Spring*, which gave rise to the environmental movement in the 1960s.

There is also an inner dimension to the path of will which a friend and colleague of mine described many years ago in a little book called *Nothing to Do with Me?*[17] In this book of essays Alexander Bos suggests that if we are upset or concerned about aspects of modern society we can ask where in my life can I find the same qualities that underlie the phenomena which trouble me? He looks at the excesses of a consumer society based on credit and debt, the impersonality of modern bureaucratic society and the monotony of modern housing developments, suggesting that we could find antidotes in our soul and act on this. We can, for example, not make significant purchases until we have the funds to do so, thereby undermining the debt-based credit card system; we can behold and make contact with the individuals serving us at the train station, the receptionist in an office, or the worker at the Department of Motor Vehicles, seeing and acknowledging them rather than treating them as objects of the bureaucratic machine. And we can examine the pattern of our lives, overcoming the monotony of routine, of uniformity by introducing more variety, and creativity, in how we live each day.

I have made it a practice, at times intermittent, to see and acknowledge the people who serve me and am surprised and delighted by the soul exchange which often happens through a genuine looking at, accompanied by a conscious thank-you. Being concerned about violence and war

I also try to not react when angry but to ponder the situation over time, working to understand the other's experience and viewpoint. I readily admit to sometimes not being able to stop my reactive self, especially with those closest to me.

I do feel that all of us have an ability to take on significant issues of our society by locating the inner quality in those issues and finding those same situations in our personal life to transform. Greed, selfishness, violence and prejudice live in us and at the same time in the world. We can practice the values of a new society in our own life, being environmentally responsible, buying food and other goods from stores whose values and policies we support, practicing non-violence in thought and deed at home and at work. We can learn to meet and value the other; our partner, our children, our colleagues and the stranger who moved in down the street. To do such work within ourselves and in our life is a powerful antidote to feelings of despair.

Some time ago a small group of friends and I began to work on issues which concerned us: racism, the election of Donald Trump, the nature of prejudice, the working of evil and climate change. We meet for four hours each month, eating a pot-luck supper together, and share the issues' impacts on our personal lives, and then explore the inner and outer dimensions of how we can work for positive change in ourselves, and in the world. This raises our awareness of the multiple dimensions of the issue, eases our sense of isolation and powerlessness and gives us courage for greater activity. It also creates a strong sense of community, as we have opened our hearts to each other. If you do not have such a group to work with on issues of common concern, I suggest you might create one.

Working for the Good

I do think we all have a greater ability to work for the good than we are normally aware of. But this requires the willingness to engage with the world, to becoming a conscious witness of our times and to overcoming two lies which the media and our society promote at every turn. The first is that you as an individual have no possibility to bring about change unless you are rich and powerful, or are part of well-organized and well-connected interest groups or organizations. The other is that your inner life, your thoughts and feelings, are irrelevant for the world. Both are manifestly untrue. It is only individuals, with the aid of others, that bring about change and progress in society. And out of our own experience we know that prayer, meditation and healing thoughts do have an effect on others and the world.

The Long Emergency of the twenty-first century can be seen as a call to our consciousness to be a witness and an active participant in shaping our society and our world. In addition to working on our own development, we have three distinct and yet deeply connected paths to practice in healing ourselves and the world, the path of insight, the journey of compassion and the path of will and transformation. They can be practiced singly or in combination but when worked with together they add depth and balance to our striving. To pick up this inner and outer work is our responsibility, our birthright and I think the path to our salvation, freeing us from the narrow confines of our egotism and making possible a new culture of compassion.

Notes

1   James Kunstler, *The Long Emergency: Surviving the Converging Catastrophes of the 21st Century*, Atlantic Monthly Press, New York, 2005. Kunstler's book is based on the notion of declining oil and energy resources and the resulting collapse of a consumer-based suburban society in the United States. He was clearly wrong about oil and yet his title and the premise of the long emergency still seem very relevant to me.
2   See Joshua Rothman, 'The Big Question: Is the world getting better or worse?', *The New Yorker*, 23 August 2018.
3   Pew Foundation Center, *World Attitudes: Is Life Better or Worse than Fifty Years Ago?*, December 2017.
4   CNN Money, 12 January 2017.
5   Mary Oliver, *Felicity*, Penguin Press, New York, 2016 – 'Late Spring', p. 69.
6   Elizabeth Kubler-Ross, *On Death and Dying: What the Dying Have to Teach Doctors, Nurses, Clergy…*, Routledge, New York, 1969. In this work Elizabeth Kubler-Ross elaborated the five stages of coming to terms with the prospect of death.
7   Martin Luther King, quoted from 'A Letter from Birmingham Jail', republished in *The Atlantic*, April 2013.
8   King James Bible, Mark 12, 28–34.
9   Quoted in Krista Tippett, Becoming Wise: *An Inquiry into the Mystery and Art of Living*, Penguin Books, New York, 2017, p. 114.
10 Nicholas Kristof and Sheryl WuDunn, *A Path Appears: Transforming Lives, Creating Opportunity*, Vintage Books, New York, 2015; and Sarah van Gelder, *The Revolution where You Live: Stories from a 12,000 Mile Journey Through a New America*, Berrett-Koehler, San Francisco, Calif., 2017.
11 Benjamin Barber, *Jihad vs. McWorld: Terrorism's Challenge to Democracy*, Time Books, New York, 1995. His argument that both terrorism and globalism are a challenge to democracy is contained in an earlier article in *The Atlantic*, March 1992.
12 John Maynard Keynes, *The General Theory of Employment, Interest and Money*, Knopf, New York, 1944, Chapter 21, pp. 383–384.
13 David Brooks, 'The axis of selfishness', *New York Times*, Friday 2 June 2017.
14 Ibid.

15 Christine Gruwez, *Walking with your time: A Manichean Journey*, Lulu, Antwerp, 2011, pp. 74–75. I have found this short book very stimulating and most helpful, along with that of Alexander Bos, *Nothing to Do with Me?* (see note 17).

16 A practice first described to me in detail by my good friend Joseph Rubano.

17 Alexander Bos, *Nothing to Do with Me? The Individual and Community*, Floris Books, Edinburgh, 1983. When I first read this book in the late 1980s, I was deeply touched because of its emphasis on the complex connections between the inner soul world and the outer world of events and actions.

Part II:

The American Empire Project

Chapter 2

The Will to Power:
The American Empire Project
(*July 2005*)

As militarism, the arrogance of power, and the euphemisms required to justify imperialism inevitably conflict with America's democratic government and distort its culture and basic values, I fear that we will lose our country.

Chalmers Johnson

Daily we are faced with grim images of road-side bombings, planned assassinations of Iraqi politicians and the killing of innocent civilians by overwhelming American firepower. How did we get into this mess, and what consequences can we draw from the disturbing pictures we see daily? This brief essay is an effort to look behind events and to chronicle the road to what Richard Falk has called the 'Global Domination Project' of the present administration.[1]

I maintain that the occupation of Iraq and Afghanistan and indeed the US 'War on Terror' is the result of a radical long-term effort on the part of political and military elites to extend American power abroad, to remake the international political order, while at the same time shaping the domestic political debate according to a neo-conservative agenda. This assertion is of course not new since observers as different as Paul Krugman and Benjamin Barber have come to similar conclusions.[2] I argue that there is a direct line of thinking and action linking the foreign policy goals of the first Bush administration with the election of 2000, the tragic events of September 11th, and the invasion of Afghanistan and Iraq under George W. Bush.

Furthermore, the costs of increased military expenditures, growing governmental deficits due to massive tax cuts, and the desire to alter Social Security and other entitlement programs constitute the domestic portion of the neo-conservative Republican agenda to remake the present political order. The groups actively supporting this shift in international and domestic politics include the Republican right, neo-conservative think tanks and groups such as the American Enterprise Institute and the Project for a New American Century, Christian Evangelicals connected to the Council for National Policy and other leaders of the Christian right. The Republicans and Democratic parties have both played into this radical takeover of US politics.

Meanwhile, the mainstream press, in particular the liberal press such as the *New York Times* and the *Washington Post*, have been relatively passive observers of a process which to my mind represents the worst elements of the American shadow; aggressive self-serving chauvinism dressed up in idealistic, moralistic and religious language. It is time to wake up to the dangers our Republic faces; politically, economically and spiritually, for the 'War on Terror' will increase terrorism, risk bankrupting our nation, and will undermine the cause of democracy at home and abroad.

The Pattern of Events

The largely self-willed and guided collapse and transformation of the Soviet Empire fundamentally changed the nature of international politics. From 1945 until 1989–90, the world was seen to be primarily bi-polar, witnessing a struggle for the hearts and minds of humanity between two ideologies: capitalism and communism, and between two Superpowers, the United States and the Soviet Union. A growing conventional and nuclear arms race led to a global struggle in which armed conflict occurred frequently, usually fought by proxy states, in developing areas. This ended in 1989–90 with the United States being perceived as the victor due to its superior economic and military power. The shift was so dramatic and unanticipated that many commentators thought that a time of peace was at hand, and even more that the triumph of liberal, democratic capitalist societies heralded the end of history, since the dialectic of competing ideologies had ended.[3]

Of course, nothing was further from the truth, and regional conflicts in Asia, Africa, Latin America, and the Middle East soon awoke the hopeful public to the continuing reality of 'wars of liberation' and 'terrorism' in its many forms.

The first Bush administration (1988–92), with Richard Cheney as Secretary of Defense and Colin Powell as head of the Joint Chiefs of Staff, found itself in the enviable position of being able to project military power without risking opposition from other nuclear states. The implications of this situation were first tested by the United States during the first Iraq War, 'Desert Storm', in which the United States and an international military coalition defeated Saddam Hussein's large conventional army after its invasion of Kuwait.

The opportunity for the global projection of American power provided by the demise of the Soviet Union led to the articulation of new defense department planning guidelines during the first Bush administration. These guidelines, known as *Defense Planning Guidance for the 1994–1999 Fiscal Years* (revised draft) Office of the Secretary of Defense 1992, and *Defense Strategy for the 1990s* (Office of the Secretary of Defense, 1993) were written for the Secretary of Defense, Richard Cheney, by Paul Wolfowitz, then under-secretary of defense for policy and Colin Powell, previously national security advisor for Ronald Reagan and now head of the Joint Chiefs of Staff for Bush. The documents depict a world dominated by the United States, which would project its economic and military power to maintain its super power status at all costs. The US would 'prevent the emergence of a new rival', would use pre-emptive force, if necessary, and would rely more on ad hoc assemblies of allies as opposed to formal alliance structures, because it was essential that America be in position 'to act independently when collective action cannot be orchestrated'.[4]

The final toned-down version of *Defense Planning Guidance* was released as *Defense Strategy for the 1990s*, just as the new Clinton administration took office. It was then to disappear from sight, but not from the minds of Cheney, Wolfowitz and Powell, who helped to see it reinstated by the Project for a New American Century in the late 1990s and then reformulated as *Defense Planning Guidance for the 2004–09 Fiscal Years* in 2002 by the second Bush administration. What had begun as an aggressive 'forward leaning' foreign policy under George Bush, reemerged in the second Bush administration altered and fueled by the shocking events of 9/11.

The Clinton years, in which US foreign policy shifted from global domination to globalism, were followed by the election of 2000, in which George W. Bush lost the popular vote by over 500,000 votes. In looking at this election, it is important to note a number of anomalies. These included that the election was decided by the Supreme Court, which blocked a re-count along strictly partisan lines, which most observers predicted would have led to a substantial Gore victory because of faulty ballots and voting machines. Secondly, 50,000 African American voters had been disenfranchised by the administration of Governor Jeb Bush, G.W. Bush's brother. And thirdly, quite remarkably, the US Senate with Al Gore in the Chair as Vice President, insisted on ratifying the vote of the Electoral College, despite numerous signed Congressional petitions from African American Congressmen and women from Florida and elsewhere, alleging voting fraud and corruption.

The election result not only assured the victory of G.W. Bush, but also of the defense and foreign policy priorities formulated by Paul Wolfowitz and Colin Powell on behalf of George Bush, and his Secretary of Defense, Richard Cheney, as the architects of these policies moved into positions of power in the new administration.

The shocking events of 9/11 allowed the second Bush administration to proceed with the aggressive defense and foreign policies previously articulated by the first Bush administration. It fulfilled a hope of the Project for a New American Century, of which Cheney, Rumsfeld and Wolfowitz were signatories, that the overthrow of Saddam Hussein's regime and the stationing of US troops in Central Asia would be possible if 'a new Pearl Harbor' were to take place. Indeed, the many unanswered questions about 9/11 have led many observers to wonder whether elements of the Administration and the military allowed 9/11 to happen as a justification for previously planned military adventures.[5]

The US military declared war on the Taliban on 7 October 2001, largely using the troops of the Northern Alliance. After many months of preparation, including the unsubstantiated linking of Saddam Hussein's regime to Al Quaeda and 9/11, and the false claim of Iraq possessing weapons of mass destruction, President Bush declared war on Iraq in April of 2003, without the support of the UN or of the international community. The wars in both Afghanistan and in Iraq are going badly, at a growing cost of military and civilian lives, and a growing governmental deficit.

The recent (as I write) election of 2004, in which John Kerry and the Democratic Party chose not to attack the record of G.W. Bush with consistency and vigor, allowed the Republicans to use the issues of fear, continuity in a time of crisis, and moral values to increase their majorities in both the House and the Senate, thereby assuring the further pursuit of existing policies.

The Strange Marriage of Machiavellian Ideas and Apocalyptic Beliefs

To understand how we have moved so quickly from being an admired nation to being feared as a threat to world peace by a large portion of humanity, it is essential to understand the ideas and beliefs which have made the Republican right so dominant.

In the area of international politics these include the ideas of Henry Kissinger, Zbigniew Brzezinski and Samuel Huntington, three of our most respected thinkers in the field of foreign policy. Each of them has contributed significantly, to shaping governmental priorities in the field of foreign affairs.

Kissinger has been the champion of the game of great power politics. In his writing and teaching he has formulated six essential principles of international politics, principles adopted by both Republican and Democratic administrations since the time of Richard Nixon and practiced by European powers in the nineteenth century.

1   A great power must have a grand, long-term global foreign policy which maximizes its interests in the world.

2   In the pursuit of such a policy, it must maintain sufficient economic and military power to defeat at least two of its rivals at any one time.

3   A great power must promote regional rivalries and conflicts, thereby always maintaining a key balancing role globally (think China–Taiwan, India–Pakistan, Israel–Palestine).

4   Democracies are not effective at the conduct of foreign policy, therefore information must be managed and true strategic interests hidden.

5   A great power must occasionally use its power overtly, otherwise the threat of force is not credible. The US involvement in military campaigns since the Second World War is legion; Korea, Vietnam, Guatemala, Chile, Panama, Nicaragua, Haiti, Yugoslavia and Lebanon, to name a few.

6   War needs to be seen not only as a natural extension of state power, but as an activity essential to the survival of the state, as articulated by the *Report from Iron Mountain* in the late 1960s.[6]

Brzezinski, the National Security Advisor of President Carter, while critical of the Iraqi War, added to Kissinger's principles of great power politics the geo-strategic objectives pursued by the United States. In the *Grand Chessboard: American Primacy and its Geostrategic Imperatives*, published in 1997, he describes the Eurasian land mass as the key to world power and control of Central Asia's oil reserves as the means to such control.[7]

Samuel Huntington, the director of the John Olin Institute of Strategic Studies, wrote a seminal article in *Foreign Affairs* in 1993 in which he characterized the emerging international order, following the demise of the Soviet Union in 1989, as consisting of a 'clash of civilizations', based on cultural and religious differences. He in particular identified Islamic cultures and the Sinic or Confucian cultures of China, Korea and Japan as well as Russia as threats to the hegemony of western cultural principles.[8]

If Kissinger described the principles of great power politics and Brzezinski the geo-political imperatives for the United States, then Huntington provided a conceptual archetype or imagination for the emerging international order. The ideas of all three men constitute an intellectual framework and justification for the foreign policy of the United States in the new millennium, and when combined with neo-conservative values and the apocalyptic beliefs of the Christian right, a powerful ideology for American domination.

While it is difficult to do justice to the complexity of Leo Strauss's political philosophy in a short essay, key tenets of his ideas have found their way into neo-conservative beliefs, for example in the writings of Irving and William Kristol, and have been used to mobilize the faithful of the Christian right. As Hugh Urban makes clear in his excellent article on 'Religion and secrecy in the Bush administration', four tenets of Staussian philosophy have found their way into the canon of neo-conservative thought:

1 the Western world, and in particular the United States, is in an intense moral crisis due to the weakness of liberal democracy;
2 the mass public cannot understand and be expected to help guide the State, therefore government and the moral elite must shield their undertakings through secrecy;
3 religion is necessary for the coherence and stability of society; and
4 rulership and government must be in the hands of gentlemen politicians 'who embody the ideals of religious faith and virtue' and 'who serve as a liaison between wise men and the common populace'.[9]

Straussian ideas and the neo-conservative movement provide a kind of intellectual bridge between the more Machiavellian and secular perspectives of Kissinger, Brzezinski and Huntington and the apocalyptic visions of the Christian right. It was after all William Kristol, Irving's son, who founded the Project for a New American Century in 1997, and Paul Wolfowitz, the Under-secretary of Defense, who was an ardent and committed student of Strauss's at the University of Chicago. Another bridging figure between the Christian right, neo-conservative thought and American foreign policy is Michael Ledeen, a fellow at the American Enterprise Institute, a favorite speaker at gatherings of the Christian right, such as Pat Robertson's 700 Club, and the author of *Machiavelli on Modern Leadership*.[10]

The centrality of religion in the life of George W. Bush is well known. It became more explicit once he decided to run for President. As he remarked to James Robinson, 'I feel like God wants me to run for President. I can't explain it, but I sense my country is going to need me.'[11] He began meeting frequently with evangelical leaders such as Jerry Falwell, Pat Robertson, Jesse Helms, Ralph Reed, Tom Delay and Tim LaHaye. Once elected in 2000, he was seen as the effective leader of the evangelical Christian movement, as well as the hope of the neo-conservative Republican right.

One third of the American public believes that the Bible is literally true, and many millions subscribe to the millennial interpretation of the Apocalypse described by LaHaye and Jenkins in the best-selling 'Left Behind' series. In this picture of coming events, after Israel has re-conquered the Holy Lands, the forces of the Anti-Christ will be defeated by Christ and his saints in a final battle at Armageddon. This victory will then usher in a new era of peace and prosperity under the direct rulership of Christ in which true Christians will be saved.[12] The time of the Apocalypse is now and George W. Bush, as the Prodigal Son and the leader of the Christian world, is seen as preparing the way for this second coming of Christ by confronting the forces of the Anti-Christ in the Middle East.

This powerful brew of Machiavellian Real Politik, neo-Conservative critiques of liberalism and millennial beliefs of an approaching Apocalypse, was given legitimacy and force by the attacks of 9/11. September 11 also made possible the Republican majority in 2004 and the continued push for global empire.

Unintended Consequences

I believe the biblical proverb of 'what you sow, you shall reap' applies to the foreign and domestic policies of the present administration. You cannot impose democracy in Iraq or Afghanistan through the barrel of a gun and you cannot defeat terrorism primarily through the exercise of state violence. We will not be successful in Iraq because too many Iraqis support the insurgents, and like in Vietnam we will be forced to withdraw. Rather than decreasing terrorism, the War in Iraq is increasing the power of militant Islam with the result that other Arab regimes such as Saudi Arabia are also being destabilized. Rather than securing future oil reserves in the Middle East, such reserves will become more uncertain. Rather than increasing our influence in the world, our aggression, hypocrisy and failure will lead to a decrease in our influence and power and make us more vulnerable to attack.

If we turn to domestic policies, and in particular the combination of economic and social policy, the same phenomenon is visible. With a trade deficit of over $400 billion and a governmental deficit of over $500 billion for this fiscal year, not counting the $200 billion that the occupation of Iraq has cost us to date, we are mortgaging our future and borrowing heavily from foreigners and future generations. The Europeans, Japanese and Chinese have increasing power over us because should they no longer be willing to hold our Treasury bills and bond the US and international financial markets would crash. And none of this takes into account the growing financial obligations that the US government has to seniors through the recently approved drug benefit programs or the entitlement programs for an aging baby boom population.[13] Politically and economically we are increasingly vulnerable. Indeed, it seems evident that we are promoting a clash of civilizations domestically and internationally while at the same time creating levels of violence, fear and instability that have an apocalyptic character. We are engaged in creating a self-fulfilling prophecy in which our policies are creating the very conditions which the administration claims to be fighting.

The Spiritual Dynamics of Fear's Empire

Benjamin Barber wrote a prescient book in 1997 titled *Jihad vs. McWorld*, in which he discussed the mutually supporting dynamic of a technologically driven materialistic global economy and a conservative, fundamentalist search for identity and meaning by those who could not or would not participate in a secular international economic order.[14] It is strange to reflect that the Republican majority has managed to bring about a marriage of these normally hostile forces through tax cuts to the wealthy and highly sophisticated political and military campaigns combined with an appeal to moral values and Christian fundamentalism.

Discernment and Hope

I would ask how we discern the integrity and authenticity of Christian prophets who seek to speak on behalf of their people as President Bush has repeatedly done. This is a man who felt called by God to political office, who has branded some nations as an Axis of Evil, who laces his speeches with a multitude of Scriptural references and who feels called upon to bring freedom as a gift from God to the Middle East.

If it is true that by their deeds you shall know them, then how do we understand a seemingly sincere man and a morally focused administration which promotes:

1   *A culture of secrecy* (the first act of the Bush administration on coming to office was to seal official records of both the Texas Governor's office and major portions of the Federal government)

2   *A culture of lies* (known falsehoods were used as a rationale for declaring war on Iraq)

3   *A culture of illusion* (a President who does not read, and is not interested in other points of view)

4   *A culture of power without compassion* (Shock and Awe, the largest short-term bombing campaign in military history, on Baghdad, the worst environmental record of recent administrations, and the torture of prisoners)

5   *A culture of belief without questions* (global warming is a myth, those who disagree with the US are abetting the enemy)

6   *A culture of fear* (in the presidential campaign, the axis of evil, the war on terror as a global commitment, orange alerts and other actions)

7   *A culture of militarism* (a General as Secretary of State, declaring victory over Iraq in a flight uniform, promoting a defense budget larger than that of all other states combined)

These to me are the signs of a false prophet, the characteristics of an incipient fascism, and the qualities associated with the unrighteous Prince of this world.

My hope lies in the arrogance and short-sightedness of power, in the fact that a sense for truth is a birthright of the human soul, and in the decency, integrity and common sense of the American people.

Notes

1   Richard Falk, *The Great Terror War*, Olive Branch Press, Northampton, Mass., 2002, p. xxvii.
2   See Paul Krugman, *The Great Unraveling – Losing our Way in the New Century*, W.W. Norton, New York, 2003, pp. 3–20; Benjamin Barber, *Fear's Empire – War, Terrorism and Democracy*, W.W. Norton, New York, 2003, pp. 16–29.
3   Frances Fukuyama, *The End of History and the Last Man*, Free Press, New York, 1992.
4   David Armstrong, 'Dick Cheney's Song of America', *Harper Magazine*, October 2002, pp. 76–83, provides a complete description of the connection between the Defense Department Planning documents of the first and second Bush administration.
5   David Ray Griffin, *The New Pearl Harbor: Disturbing Questions about the Bush Administration and 9/11*, Olive Branch Press, Northampton, Mass., 2004.
6   As taught by Henry Kissinger in the National Security Seminar at Harvard in 1966, and in *Diplomacy*, Simon and Schuster, New York, 1994, pp. 17–28 and 703–836.
7   Zbigniew Brzezinski, *The Grand Chessboard, American Primacy and its Geostrategic Imperatives*, Basic Books, New York, 1997, pp. xii–xv, 195–205.
8   See Samuel Huntington, *The Clash of Civilizations and the Remaking of World Order*, Simon and Schuster, New York, 2003; in particular, pp. 125–174 and 207–238.
9   Hugh Urban, 'Religion and secrecy in the Bush administration: The gentlemen, the prince and simulacrum', Esoterica; also available on the internet under Hugh Urban, pp. 6–7, pp. 14–15, 17–22.
10 Michael Ledeen, *Machiavelli on Modern Leadership: Why Machiavelli's Iron Rules are as Timely Today as Five Centuries Ago*, St Martin's Press, New York, 1999.
11 Quoted in Urban, op. cit, p. 4.
12 See Tim LaHaye and Jerry B. Jenkins, *Glorious Appearing, the End of Days*, Tyndale House Publishers, Wheaton, Ill., 2004.
13 See Krugman, op. cit, pp. xv–xxix, and 3–26.
14 Benjamin R. Barber, *Jihad vs McWorld: Terrorism's Challenge to Democracy*, Random House, New York, 1995.

Chapter 3

Disturbing Questions about 9/11 and the War on Terror (*October 2004*)

One year later, the public knows less about the circumstances of 2,801 deaths at the foot of Manhattan in broad daylight than people in 1912 knew within weeks about the Titanic.

New York Times, 9 November 2002

There are endless questions one can ask about events since the first Bush administration took office in 1988 leading up to the election of 2000 and to 9/11 and its consequences. I will limit myself to those which to my mind are most essential, and to provide some commentary. My purpose in raising these questions is to help the reader deepen their own reflections and arrive at their own conclusions about the period between 1989 and the present (2004).

1 Why was there not a broad bi-partisan and national debate about the aims of US foreign policy following the transformation and collapse of the Soviet Union?

While some discussions did occur in Congress about decreasing military expenditure, a sustained dialogue devoted to rethinking the possibilities for global peace and improved global prosperity, or of changing the principles of the grand chess game of international politics, did not occur. Nor was this called for by either the liberal or conservative press or by most academicians. Instead, Cheney as Sect. of Defense, and Colin Powell as Head of the Joint Chiefs of Staff and others in the administration of

G.W. Bush were intent on finding justifications for continuing large-scale defense expenditures and for capitalizing on the unchallenged primacy of the United States. This resulted in *The Defense Strategy for the 1990s* (1993), providing the later basis for the unilateral policies of the second Bush administration.[1]

2   How was it possible for the attack-dog politics of Newt Gingrich and other conservative Republicans to appeal to the American public?
A connected question is, how was it even conceivable that the House and the Senate initiated impeachment proceedings against President Clinton for his dalliance with a White House intern when no one has been held accountable for the far more serious untruths of the second Bush administration about the reasons for going to war in Iraq or the supposed intelligence failures leading up to it? The passive acceptance of both the attack-dog tactics of conservative Republicans in the 1990s, and of impeachment proceedings against Bill Clinton, was a main cause for the electoral success of George W. Bush in the election of 2000, and for the reinstatement of the foreign policy goals of the first Bush administration during the second.

3   What really happened in the presidential election of 2000?
Why did the Supreme Court block any recount effort by a partisan 5:4 majority? Why did not one Senator, including Ted Kennedy, support the efforts of black Congressmen and women from Florida to legally block the electoral count, citing as they did, documented cases of systematic voting fraud and irregularities for African American voters? Why did the press, the Democratic Party and the voters accept an election result which violated the principle of one person, one vote, and why did we all turn a blind eye to likely election fraud by Republican Party operatives? To make these questions even more specific and poignant, why did not one major US newspaper carry articles published in reputable European papers describing the systematic deletion of African American voters from the voter rolls in Florida and other states in the election of 2000.

Without the election of G. W. Bush, it is highly unlikely that the neo-conservative foreign policy agenda of the first Bush administration would have been pursued by the United States under Gore. Perhaps even 9/11 could have been averted, given the testimony of Richard Clarke who has systematically maintained that the Clinton administration gave a higher priority to Al-Qaeda and fighting terrorism than the new Bush administration.[2]

4   Why did the CIA and the FBI do such a poor job in following the intelligence leads that were provided for 12 of the 18 hijackers who took part in 9/11?

To say that the CIA failed to pass on the information to the FBI and that the FBI could not connect the dots seems ludicrous, given the amount of money spent on intelligence and the warnings provided by FBI station heads and agents. The 9/11 Commission Report concludes, 'no one looked at the bigger picture and connected the intelligence or the individual hijackers to the growing terrorist warnings'.[3] Why not?

5   Why were the 38 intelligence warnings given to the USA by foreign governments and the CIA, and the 6 August 2001 presidential briefing on the threat from Al-Qaeda, not responded to by heightened FBI and airline security (FAA) measures when, as George Tenet, the former CIA chief, noted, the system was blinking red?

No special precautions were taken in the summer and early autumn of 2001 despite ample warning of Al Queda's intention to attack targets within the USA. The 9/11 Commission Report states that 'across the government there were failures of imagination, policy, capabilities and management', but it does not explore whether willful omissions occurred. Nor does it blame US foreign policy, or the one-sided US support of Israel as contributing factors in the growth of terrorism.[4]

6   Why were none of the four hijacked airliners intercepted by F-15s and, if need be, shot down by NORAD (North American Aerospace Defense Command)? Why did the FAA take so long to notify NORAD of the hijackings?

Standard Operating Procedure is for traffic controllers of the FAA to notify the military of suspected hijackings as soon as possible and for NORAD to scramble planes to intercept flights that are either off course or hijacked. Standard Operating Procedures would have suggested an intercept within 10 minutes of notification. The first flight, American Airlines #11, left Boston at 7:59 a.m., and failed to respond to an order from the FAA at 8:14 a.m. This was followed by a detailed ongoing communication by a stewardess with an AA reservation desk at 9.18, in which she described the unfolding of the hijacking. The FAA controller definitely knew of the hijacking by 8.25 a.m., but fighter planes were not scrambled until 8.46, as Standard Operating Procedures were not followed. United Airlines flight #175 from Boston to LAX departed at 8.14 a.m., and the hijackers attacked between 8.42 and 8.46. At 8.51 and 8.52 it was known that Flight 175 had been hijacked, still eleven minutes before it struck the South Tower at 9.03. NORAD was not notified until 9.03, according to the 9/11 Commission Report.[5]

American Airlines flight #77 which, according to the Report, crashed into the Pentagon at 9.38 was not clearly identified as a hijacked airliner until 9.23, and the scrambled aircraft from Langley left at 9.33, without any clear indication of the hijacked airliner's location or direction. Indeed, the FAA had not even asked for help from NORAD with American flight 77.

United Airlines flight #93, which crashed in Pennsylvania at around 10.03 a.m., also was not intercepted, with a similar tale of inadequate co-ordination and response.

The Commission report concludes, 'The defense of U.S. airspace on 9/11 was not conducted in accord with pre-existing training and protocols'.[6] It does not assign blame, nor inquire into why this was the case.

Critics of the official account point to FAA regulations which state that an emergency exists when there is an unexpected loss of radar contact and radio communication with any aircraft. It instructs controllers that 'if you are in doubt, handle it as though it were an emergency'.[7] According to spokespeople from the FCC and NORAD, it normally takes a minute or two for the FAA to contact NORAD and the National Military Command Center (NMCC), and a few minutes for fighter jets to be scrambled. The tardy and inadequate response of both the FAA, the NMCC and NORAD has led skeptics to argue that the tale of incompetence and missed opportunities is too extensive to be credible, much like the intelligence failures of the FBI and the CIA. They suggest that a 'stand down order' from the commander of NORAD, or the Secretary of Defense, would have been required to block Standard Operating Procedures. It is interesting to note that no FAA nor NORAD personnel were dismissed as a result of inadequate or improper emergency responses connected to the events of 9/11. Nor did the Commission explore the possibility of official complicity in the failed responses to the hijackings.

7   Did the twin towers of the World Trade Center collapse because of the two airplane crashes and the igniting of fuel in the towers?
The Federal Emergency Management Agency (FEMA), in its report of May 2002, stated that the 'sequence of events leading to the collapse of each tower could not be definitely determined'.[8] The normal assumption and explanation of the collapse is that fire, fueled by jet fuel, melted the steel girders of the towers, leading to their collapse. However, as numerous

skeptics have argued, to melt steel requires a temperature of 1,500 degrees Celsius or 2,770 degrees Fahrenheit. Hydrocarbon fuels burn at 1,600 to 1,700 F. As David Griffin argues, for the official theory to be credible, there must have been moderately hot fires, spread throughout the building and burning for a long time. All the evidence suggests that this was not the case. Some critics therefore argue that the towers collapsed because of a controlled demolition through set explosives.

8   Why did the WTC Building 7 collapse?

Set over 350 feet away from the towers and not hit by significant debris, building 7 caught on fire and collapsed at 5.20 p.m. Even with the stored fuel in the basement, WTC 7 would be the 'first steel-framed building in history to collapse solely from fire damage'.[9] FEMA found no good explanation for this collapse.

9   What was the President doing at the Sarasota, Florida grammar school when all evidence suggests he knew about Flight 11's crash into the World Trade Center before entering the building?

By 8.48, the first pictures of the World Trade Center fire were being broadcast. Shortly after entering the school the President was updated by Condoleezza Rice, and still he chose to sit with a group of school children. As James Bamford notes,

> Having just been told that the country was under attack, the Commander in Chief appeared uninterested in further details. He never asked if there had been any additional threats, where the attacks were coming from, how to best protect the country from further attacks.... Instead in the middle of a modern day Pearl Harbor, he simply turned back to the matter at hand, the day's photo opportunity.[10]

Remarkable behavior for the President of the United States at the defining moment of his presidency.

10   Why did the US government permit the secret evacuation of Saudi Arabians and members of the Bin Laden family immediately after 9/11?

While it is stated that Richard Clarke, Bush's anti-terrorism czar, approved the Saudi government's requests to evacuate Saudi citizens and bin Laden family members, it is nevertheless striking that such an airlift happened and that the interrogation of the departing Saudi's was very limited. This air evacuation is all the more remarkable, given the large number of Saudi hijackers involved in 9/11, and the known relationships between Al Queda, Osama bin Laden and the house of Saud.

11   Were Osama bin Laden and Al-Qaeda solely responsible for 9/11 or were there other important players in this tragedy?

David Griffin reports that John O'Neill, a counter-terrorism expert for the FBI, resigned in August 2001, citing repeated obstruction by the White House in investigating Al Queda. O'Neill stated, 'Bin Laden and his gang are just the tentacles of the Wahhabi octopus, the head lies safely in Saudi Arabia, protected by U.S. forces'.[11] The close relation between the bin Laden family, the Saudi royal family and the Bush administration is well known, but has received little scrutiny. All indications are that such investigations were killed by the administration.[12] The same is true of the connection between the CIA, the Pakistan intelligence service, ISI, the Taliban and Al Queda.

12   Why was there such a minimal critical investigation by the mass media of the events of 9/11?

I have already pointed to the comment in the *New York Times* and the *Philadelphia Daily News* that remarkably so little was known about 9/11, one and even two years after the event. No mainstream paper or magazine has directly questioned the official account, despite many anomalies and unanswered questions. Given the popularity of Michael Moore's *Fahrenheit 911*, it surely isn't for lack of public interest. No doubt the public pressure and the fear of being branded unpatriotic have played a role, especially as the President proclaimed on 14 September 2001, 'Our responsibility to history is already clear; to answer these attacks and rid the world of evil'.[13] Perhaps more importantly, to challenge the official account is to contemplate government complicity in the attacks of 9/11, a direction few people want to consider because of what it would imply about our society and our political system.

13   Why was an international legal or political response to Al Queda's attack on 9/11 not considered by the administration as opposed to an invasion of Afghanistan?

It could be argued that given the emotion surrounding the tragedy of 9/11, a military response was a necessity or that the pursuit of legal or political means would be too slow. But perhaps other factors played a role as Seymour Hersh and others have pointed out, as the presence of US forces and a friendly regime in Afghanistan would secure the long-planned oil pipeline from the Caspian Sea through Afghanistan and Pakistan to the

Arabian Sea, providing much-needed oil to the insatiable economies of the USA and China.

14   Why was the hunt for Osama bin Laden so lackluster and ineffective, both before and after 9/11?

Not only were repeated plans to capture or destroy bin Laden cancelled, but there is reliable evidence that bin Laden was in an American hospital in Dubai in July of 2001 and was even visited by a local CIA agent, Larry Mitchell.[14] A number of European newspapers reported this explosive story, but it was not picked up by the US media. Perhaps one needs to consider that the continued existence of bin Laden as a personification of evil justifies the 'War on Terror', the increased military expenditure and the occupation of Afghanistan and Iraq.

15   Why did the administration oppose the creation of the 9/11 Commission and then, when finally forced to respond because of pressure from survivors' families, suggest Henry Kissinger as the Commission's chairperson?

And a connected question: why didn't Congress insist on an independent commission not consisting of presidential appointees?

16   If Al-Qaeda and the Taliban were public enemy number one, why did the USA commit so few forces to Afghanistan, and then drain off the most experienced for the invasion of Iraq?

The United States has at no point had more than 20,000 troops in Afghanistan and has, according to many observers, committed limited resources to the capture of bin Laden.

17   Why did the USA need to invade Iraq in the Spring of 2003 when it was clear to most knowledgeable observers that Iraq did not pose a threat to US national security, and had no known links to al Queda?

Part of the rationale for this step was previously discussed, namely that Cheney, Powell, Rumsfeld and Wolfowitz saw the necessity of a US invasion of Iraq before 9/11, and even before the election of 2000.

The rationale provided to the American public for the invasion included:

1   Saddam Hussein's regime possessed extensive stockpiles of chemical and biological weapons.
2   Iraq was working to develop nuclear weapons and acquire enriched uranium from other countries.

3   Iraq had active links to Al-Qaeda and other terrorist organizations, and would provide them with weapons of mass destruction.
4   The regime of Saddam Hussein was a brutal dictatorship murdering and suppressing its own people.
5   The Iraqis would welcome US troops with open arms.
6   It was essential to establish a new democratic regime in Iraq to provide a model for other Arab states, and to relieve pressure on Israel.

All of the reasons provided were false, with the exception of the brutality of Saddam Hussein's regime. Some of them were known to be false at the time of the US invasion, such as the effort by Iraq to acquire materials for atomic weapons from Africa, and the existence of active links between Al-Qaeda and Iraq. Colin Powell's persuasive presentation at the UN was largely based on misinformation. To what degree he was involved in a conscious deception is an open question.

18   Can we really believe that the mainstream media had no inkling about the false pretenses being used by the Bush administration to justify the invasion of Iraq?
Both the media and the US Congress took the statements by the administration about the threat of Iraq at face value, despite knowing of the intense pressure which Cheney, Bush and others were putting on the CIA to find linkages between Al-Qaeda and Iraq, and despite the testimony of UN inspectors that there were no WMD in Iraq. The recent admission of failures in editorial policy in the *New York Times* and *The Washington Post* regarding the rationales for the invasion of Iraq does little to reassure a critical observer.

19   Did the US government not know that the largely unilateral, pre-emptive use of force in Iraq over the opposition of our key allies and of the UN would lead to a great loss of international respect and support?
World public opinion is not negligible. The American invasion of Iraq created the largest series of coordinated international war protests in history. The opposition of Germany and France and the suspicions of Russia, not to mention the negative reaction of Muslims worldwide, are a high price to pay for such a costly military adventure with such an uncertain outcome. Indeed, it can be argued that the invasion of Iraq was calculated to increase terrorism, and to magnify religious and cultural differences between Christian and Muslim nations, rather than the reverse.

20   Could the pattern of events since the defeat of George Bush in 1992 to the victory of George W. Bush in 2000, and up to the tragedy of 9/11 and the invasions of Afghanistan and Iraq, reflect a planned manifestation of the 'will to power' by political and economic elites in the United States?

The most inflammatory aspect of such a question is the thought of active collusion and participation in the events of 9/11 by decision makers in the Bush administration. However, I believe the questions must be asked because the anomalies, failures and direct lies attending 9/11, and the many tardy governmental responses, reflect a level of incompetence and a willful disregard of the truth which defies the imagination. Put another way, the collusion, if not active participation, of key figures in the US government in the events of 9/11 provides a better, and more credible, explanation of what happened than to assume an astounding level of incompetence and mismanagement at all levels of government.

It is important to note that collusion or complicity can mean many things: from some intelligence operatives knowing that something like 9/11 would eventually happen, thus providing a golden opportunity to garner support for a pre-existing defense and foreign policy (benign neglect), to active CIA, Pentagon, or White House involvement in this egregious act of terrorism. I agree with David Ray Griffin that the facts suggest strong evidence for some form of official complicity, without knowing how extensive or active such complicity was.[15]

The main argument against such a case is the extraordinary risk and arrogance which such acts of complicity would imply; for it would suggest a willingness on the part of many individuals to not feel compelled to tell the truth and for the 'free press' to not question official accounts. Can one assume that this happened? Perhaps, given the record of four administrations in hiding the recognition that Vietnam was not a winnable war, or the still-existing questions about politically motivated murders of key political figures such as John F. Kennedy and Martin Luther King Jr. In any case, an Independent Commission of Inquiry into 9/11, chartered by Congress, would go a long way to easing the mind of skeptical observers since the attacks of 9/11 provided the perfect rationale for unfolding the previously planned projection of military force in the Middle East.

Present-day Commentary *(October 2017)*

Since raising these questions in 2004 and discussing them with various other observers, I have not heard or read anything that provides clear answers. No independent commission, free of government control, has been created to look at the events of 9/11, despite the efforts of the survivor's families, and no well-known journal or newspaper has dared to raise any serious objections to the official government account about what happened on 9/11. I remain skeptical of governmental accounts and rationales.

Meanwhile David Jay Griffin, a well-known professor of theology, on whom I relied heavily for this list of pertinent questions and concerns in this essay, has gone on to write other logical and evidence-based critiques of the Bush/Cheney administration, and of the 9/11 Commission Report. In addition to *The New Pearl Harbor*, he has published *The 9/11 Commission Report: Omissions and Distortions* (2004), *Bush and Cheney: How They Ruined America and the World* (2017), and *The New Pearl Harbor Revisited* (2004). An organization called Architects and Engineers for 9/11 Truth exists, and has created and promoted a movie called '9/11 Blueprint for Truth', arguing that only a controlled demolition could have brought down all three buildings of the World Trade Center. Many other sources have argued for some sort of US and/or Israeli complicity. It would not be the first time the US government and its intelligence services have masterminded a false-flag incident, including the alleged attack in the Gulf of Tonkin, leading to the escalation of the Vietnam War.

Notes

1 *Defense Strategy for the 1990s* (1993), quoted from David Armstrong, 'Dick Cheney's song of America', *Harper Magazine*, October 2002, pp. 76–79.

2 Richard Clark, *Against All Enemies: Inside America's War on Terror*, Free Press, New York, 2003. pp. 241–242.

3 *The 9/11 Commission Report*, Government Printing Office, Washington, D.C., 2003, p. 277.

4 Ibid., p. 276.

5 Ibid., see pp. 1–14 of the Commission Report for a detailed time description of the four flights.

6 Ibid., p. 23.

7 Quoted in David Ray Griffin, *The New Pearl Harbor: Disturbing Questions about the Bush Administration and 9/11*, Olive Branch Press, Northampton, Mass., 2004, p. 4. Most of the questions raised in this short essay have been adapted from this excellent and thorough study by David Griffin. Indeed, his books have been a major source of inspiration for me in putting together this series of essays.

8 Ibid., p. 12.

9 Quoted in Griffin, p. 14.

10   Ibid., p. 21.
11   Ibid., quoted on p. 59.
12   Quoted in Griffin, p. 78.
13   President's remarks at the National Day of Prayer and Remembrance, 14 September 2001.
14   Asserted in *Le Figaro*, 31 October 2001, in The *Guardian*, 1 November 2001, and in the London *Times*, 1 November 2001.
15   See Griffin, p. xxiv.

Part III:

The Crisis of Western Capitalism

Chapter 4

The Crisis of Western Capitalism
(October 2009)

...soon or late it is ideas, not vested interests, which are dangerous for good or evil.

John Maynard Keynes

It is now clear that the global economy is facing the worst crisis since the Great Depression. Unemployment is rising rapidly in all countries, with effective unemployment and under-employment in the USA reaching 12 per cent. The United States, the engine of global economic expansion during the last decade, has been in recession since the last quarter of 2007, with both Europe and Asia feeling the effect of declining exports. The magnitude and the duration of the economic crisis is still uncertain, but the size of the projected deficit for 2009 is expected to exceed $1 trillion, while the total bailout and economic stimulus package has been estimated to be over $7 trillion – $25,000 for every person in the United States today. This enormous effort to breathe life into a failing economy, while heroic, is also a burden to future generations, and promises to create conditions of austerity for many Americans for years to come.

The immediate cause of the crisis is understood to be the failure of the sub-prime mortgage market and the related drop in home prices, but the true causes go much deeper: the deregulation of the financial markets beginning with Ronald Reagan, the easy money and low interest rate policies of the Federal Reserve under Alan Greenspan and his successors, the reckless and corrupt behavior of financial institutions and Wall Street firms, and most importantly, the increase in private, corporate and governmental debt during the last eight years of the Bush Aadministration.

Total outstanding US debt, private and public, had grown from $2 trillion in 1974 to over $44 trillion in 2006, and has increased markedly since then.

While there is considerable discussion of the economic and financial crisis there is yet scant recognition that we are witnessing a crisis of Western capitalism: of the way in which American society is organized and functions. With the fall of the communist regime in Russia and Eastern Europe in 1989–90, there were many self-congratulatory statements in the American press about the triumph of market capitalism and of the American way of life, as well as much disparagement of the social democracies of Western Europe. Now it is our turn to undergo critical scrutiny, as the rest of the world quite rightly sees that the excesses of our financial markets have caused the global economic crisis, as they did during the Great Depression in the late 1920s.

John Maynard Keynes, the great British economist, remarked on a number of occasions that economic and social ideas matter, for they determine the realities we create. As quoted earlier, he also added, 'soon or late, it is ideas, not vested interests, which are dangerous for good or evil'. So let us look at the ideas which lie at the heart of the free-market ideology, triumphant both in economics and more generally in the social sciences since the time of Ronald Reagan and Margaret Thatcher.

The ideology of free-market capitalism is called neoliberalism and dates back to the work of Friedrich Hayek and Ludwig von Mises, both Austrian exiles who despised the social democracy of the interwar years and its fascist enemies. In *The Road to Serfdom* (Hayek) and *Bureaucracy* (von Mises), it is argued that competition and struggle are the defining characteristics of human relationships, that people are primarily consumers, and that competition and the market maximize human and social well-being. This ideology was quickly supported by wealthy business elites on both sides of the Atlantic and by the new conservative think tanks, such as the Cato Institute, the Heritage Foundation and the American Enterprise Institute. The ideology was quite naturally embraced by the Republican party in the USA and by the Tories in the UK, becoming the basis of the Reagan and Thatcher revolution.

Free-market economists such as Milton Friedman and his students at the University of Chicago further elaborated this 'efficient market hypothesis', arguing that stock, bond and other prices most accurately reflect what is known and knowable about the fundamentals of the economy and that efficient markets, unfettered by government control, will do the best job of allocating jobs and financial resources to promote economic growth.

Combined with the libertarian ideas of limited government, the pro-business orientation of the Republican party and the political ideals of the neo-conservative movement, neoliberal ideas represented a powerful ideology for shrinking government, reducing taxes, privatizing services, deregulating markets and globalizing economic activity. They also justified a heartless approach to the poor, the unemployed, the old and the disadvantaged, for if you are not doing well it's your fault for lacking the education, the skills or the ability to thrive in a meritocracy. After all, we are the land of opportunity, even if millions of jobs have been shipped overseas, and the official unemployment rate stands at 14 per cent.

The principles of neoliberal ideology were succinctly summarized by David Korten in *When Corporations Rule the World*:

- sustained economic growth as measured by the Gross Domestic Product, is the path to human progress.
- free markets, unrestrained by government, generally result in the most efficient and socially optimal allocation of resources.
- economic globalization, achieved by removing barriers to the free flow of goods and money anywhere in the world, spurs competition, increases economic efficiency, creates jobs, lowers consumer prices, increases consumer choice, increases economic growth and is generally beneficial to almost everyone.
- privatization, which moves functions and assets from government to the private sector, improves efficiency.
- the primary responsibility of government is to provide the infrastructure necessary to advance commerce and enforce the rule of law with respect to property rights and contracts.[1]

These principles rest on a set of assumptions which, when articulated, reveal their extraordinary one-sidedness:

1   People are motivated by self-interest, expressed through the quest for financial gain.
2   The actions taken by individuals and groups to maximize their financial gain bring the greatest benefit to society.
3   Social and economic life is characterized by competition rather than co-operation, and society is best organized around this principle.
4   Human progress is best measured by the consumption and production of goods and services as expressed in the Gross Domestic

Product, (GDP), even when such measures include pollution clean-up, or weapon replacement.

5   Economic activity is the primary purpose of society.

I will comment briefly on some of the principles and assumptions of the free-market, neoliberal ideology of the Republican party and of many business elites, before mentioning some possibilities for the future. The first and most important reservation is that human beings are not only engaged in work and economic acquisition, that society contains cultural meaning and life – plays, novels, concerts and museums – which have nothing to do with maximizing our economic advantage, and also includes a political and social life, of relationships and associations, of voting and exercising our rights as citizens. A second limitation of the free-market ideology is that its perspective on markets is myopic. While markets do many things well, without government regulation, capital and labor markets produce severe distortions, as Robert Kuttner has shown in *Everything for Sale: The Virtues and Limitations of Markets*, and as the present financial crisis demonstrates.

Another significant issue to consider is the inappropriateness of the Gross Domestic Product (GDP) as a way of measuring societal health and progress. While the United States is considered to be the wealthiest country in the world, it is ranked behind many other advanced industrial societies in terms of quality of life and social health, as described in my essay on income inequalities.

Then there is the question of competition, of organizing society around competition and selfishness as the primary motive of action. We know that the informal-care economy of raising children and of tending to the sick and the elderly is a huge and unrecognized part of social and economic activity. It is not based on either competition or economic reward: it is based on mutual service and support, and without it society would surely collapse.

Rudolf Steiner, the Austrian philosopher and writer, suggested that societies based on egotism and greed would be characterized by suffering, poverty and want, and would spread those qualities globally because of the exploitative nature of the individual and societal consciousness produced. Has this not happened? Do the wars in the Middle East, the famines in Africa and the growing environmental disasters not reflect the material-istic, exploitative nature of the global capitalistic system?

Already at the end of the nineteenth century, Prince Kropotkin's classic study *Mutual Aid* showed how co-operation, both in the natural and human world, produces the healthiest communities and societies. Neither the massive destruction and suffering of the twentieth century, nor the evidence of a growing dysfunctionality in the economic and political systems of the West, has moved us to seriously look at other options.

To restore American society to the promise of its founders and to renew the social contract between government and its citizens, it is essential to limit the power of financial and business interests. Otherwise we will continue to have the 'best democracy money can buy'. A recent article in *The Atlantic* by Simon Johnson, previously the chief economist at the IMF, persuasively argues that the USA, like Russia under Putin, or like many developing societies, has developed a form of 'crony capitalism' in which the financial sector has undue influence so that it can shield itself from the consequences of its own reckless behavior by receiving a very favorable bailout at the taxpayer's expense.

The public financing of elections and the barring of private or group donations to political parties and campaigns constitute the most important step which can be taken to avoid the plutocracy we now have where one dollar/one vote is replacing the principle of one person/one vote. Secondly, the national and international regulation of financial markets, banking and the credit card and insurance industries is necessary to avoid the speculation, corruption and undue influence of the financial sector. If the public bails them out, government has the right to regulate and to prohibit financial instruments such as derivatives or activities such as short selling, which do not contribute to healthy economic growth. Research and rethinking is required in financial markets in order to distinguish between what Kevin Phillips calls 'bad money', which is purely speculative in nature, and 'good money', which fosters the balanced and sustainable production of goods and services.

The most important decision-maker of the economic system in the United States is the Federal Reserve. As an institution and a Board which represents the twelve federal reserve banks, it serves the needs of capital and the financial markets first and those of ordinary citizens second, as William Greider has shown so eloquently in his study, *Secrets of the Temple*. It needs to be made more democratically accountable, with at least half of its members representing the public, not the banks.

A further step in balancing the excessive power of corporations and finance is to consider corporate charter reform so that the right of person-hood, granted to corporations by the states, is not permanent, but is reviewed every ten years using the criteria of the triple bottom line; profit, environmental sustainability and community responsibility.

If the present financial crisis leads to asking fundamental questions of how American society can become more democratic, can indeed become a society of 'liberty and justice for all', then the crisis will have been used well and will lead to a society in which an activist government serves the public good and promotes cultural freedom and diversity, equality in all aspects of political and social life, and an economy which serves human needs in an environmentally sustainable way.

General Reference Notes
William Greider, *Secrets of the Temple: How the Federal Reserve Runs the Country*, Simon and Schuster, New York, 1995.
William Greider, *The Soul of Capitalism: Opening Paths to a Moral Economy*, Simon and Schuster, New York, 2004.
Simon Johnson, 'The quiet coup', *The Atlantic*, May 2009.
David Korten, *When Corporations Rule the World*, Kumerian, Berret-Koehler, San Francisco, 1995, pp. 70–71. This is listed as footnote 1.
David Korten, *The Post-Corporate World, 2000*, Berrett-Koehler, San Francisco, 2004.
Robert Kuttner, *Everything for Sale: The Virtues and Limits of Markets*, Knopf, New York, 1996.
Kevin Phillips, *Bad Money, Reckless Finance, Failed Politics and the Global Crisis of American Capitalism*, Viking, New York, 2009.
Katrina van den Heuvel, *Meltdown: How Greed and Corruption Shattered our Financial System and How We Can Recover*, Nation Books, Washington, 2009.

Chapter 5

Reflections on the Global Economic Crisis and What to Do About It: A Journey through the Dismal Science *(October 2014)*

> Bad money drives out good money and bad capitalism drives out good.
>
> Gresham's Law (updated)

This multi-year reflection on the global economic crisis describes a variety of books that I have found informative in making sense of our present predicament. It includes social and political perspectives without which the economic issues lack context and meaning. It is also an invitation to immerse oneself in some of the best thinking in alternative economics and to use your money more locally and wisely.

- The first book, by David Korten, *When Corporations Rule the World* (Berrett-Koehler, 1995) describes the marauding tactics of global corporations in bending national governments and international agencies to their will, while maximizing their profits and destroying both cultural and natural environments. It provides a good context for understanding the globalization movement and the principles and tactics of free-market capitalism.
- In 2008, just at the beginning of the American and then the later global economic meltdown, Kevin Phillips published *Bad Money: Reckless Finance, Failed Politics and the Global Crisis of American Capitalism* (Penguin, 2008). This entertaining and depressing study reveals the thoughts and actions of Wall Street moguls and their

political henchman in Washington, D.C., both Democrats and Republicans. It provides a detailed case study of how most of our institutions failed us, from the watchdog agencies, such as the SEC (Securities and Exchange Commission), the rating agencies (Standard and Poor's), to our political representatives in controlling the excesses of the financial sector. Phillips demonstrates the truth of Gresham's Law, 'Bad money drives out good money, or bad capitalism tends to drive out the good and not the reverse'. He also points out that the financial services sector has grown to represent 20–21 per cent of the Gross Domestic Product in the USA, while manufacturing has shrunk to 13 per cent, as many jobs have been shipped overseas, benefitting the large corporations but devastating the industrial heartland of America.

- A deeper look at the intersection of politics and economics is provided by the very insightful and polemical reader, *The Global Economic Crisis: The Great Depression of the 21st Century* (Global Research, 2010), edited by Michel Chossudovsky and Andrew Gavin Marshall. This comprehensive volume covers a great deal of territory, as shown by the table of contents, Part I: The Global Economic Crisis; Part II: Global Poverty; Part III: War, National Security and World Government; Part IV: The Global Monetary System; and Part V: The Shadow Banking System. The essays place most of the blame for current world problems on the United States because of its drive for global domination. The book's often strident tone is unfortunately seldom relieved by clear suggestions for transformation.

- For a more conventional but still very far-reaching analysis, see Joseph Stiglitz, *Free-fall: America, Free Markets, and the Sinking of the World Economy* (W.W. Norton, 2010). Stiglitz has also written an excellent study of the reasons behind the growing disparity of wealth in the United States and how neither political reform nor economic recovery is possible without addressing such inequalities. See *The Price of Inequality: How Today's Divided Society Endangers our Future* (W.W. Norton, 2012). Robert Reich makes a very similar point in looking at stagnant wages since the late 1970s and the toxic excess of income inequalities, which led to the indebtedness of the American consumer, in *Aftershock: The Next Economy and America's Future* (Alfred A. Knopf, 2010). He argues that the United States has forgotten the lessons of the Great Depression, that everyone needs to benefit from increases in productivity, otherwise there cannot be economic recovery, since the 99 per cent will not have the purchasing power to support the growth of consumption.

- Christopher Houghton Budd's book *Finance at the Threshold: Rethinking the Real and Financial Economics* (Gower, 2012) is full of intriguing ideas and challenges to mainstream economics. It locates the fundamental problem of the world economy in the excess liquidity of global financial markets; too many dollars or yen chasing too few opportunities for profitable investments. His answer to this problem, relying on ideas in Rudolf Steiner's *World Economy*, would be to vastly increase the amount economic life gifts to the young, to education and to culture, thereby enhancing creativity and innovation in all sectors of society, as well as decreasing excess liquidity. Another essential insight is the recognition that a global economic system requires global economic thinking and a global currency, such as bancor, advocated by John Maynard Keynes at the end of the Second World War.

- David Korten, in early 2009, just as the Obama presidency was beginning, wrote a compelling account of how the economy could be transformed, including abolishing Wall Street, reclaiming the right of issuing corporate charters and forcing companies to implement the triple bottom line; economic viability, environmental sustainability and community responsibility. The book, *Agenda for a New Economy* (Berrett-Koehler, 2009), was largely ignored by politicians and the mainstream press, as it questioned too many assumptions of the underlying capitalistic order.

- Then there is the hopeful and moving book by Charles Eisenstein, *Sacred Economics: Money, Gift and Society in the Age of Transition* (Evolver, 2011). His argument is deceptively simple but difficult to grasp. Simple, because he, like Steiner, sees the fundamental problem of market-driven economics as being the interest-bearing nature of money, and the existence of private land ownership as opposed to common ownership of land and natural resources. Difficult, because to think in new ways about money, price, land, work and income, requires freeing ourselves from the taken for granted 'truths' of modern economics which so permeate our culture. For example he states,

> The urge to own grows as a natural response to an alienating ideology that severs felt connections and leaves us alone in the universe. When we exclude world from self, the tiny, lonely identity

that remains has a voracious need to claim as much as possible of that lost beingness for its own sake. If all the world, all of life and earth is no longer me, I can at least compensate by making it mine. Other separate selves do the same, so we live in a world of competition and omnipresent anxiety.

Eisenstein's solutions in the section called 'The Economics of Reunion' include negative interest-bearing currency which devalues if not spent, eliminating rents and interest, compensating for the depletion of the commons, and taking steps to providing a Guaranteed Basic Income. Read this book if you are looking for inspiration and some hope, and then add Martin Large's *Common Wealth: For a Free, Equal, Mutual and Sustainable Society* (Hawthorn Press, 2012), for many examples of how a tri-sectoral or three-fold approach to economic and social questions is already emerging in Western societies. Finally, add Steiner's *World Economy* (Rudolf Steiner Press), and Gary Lamb's *Associative Economics* (AWSNA) and you have the basis of a new economics curriculum and a description of what I believe to be a path toward a healthier economy and society.

I think there are four fundamental issues which need to be resolved before the world will be able to experience an equitable economy which does not destroy the earth and create unbearable inequities and suffering. The first of these is that our money system should not be based on debt. At present, in the United States and most other countries, a central bank, in our case the Federal Reserve, loans money to banks at a set interest rate. The regular commercial banks then turn around and loan money out, far in excess of what they have actually borrowed from the Fed, and at a still higher interest. Because they engage in this fractional reserve banking, loaning out much more than they have in reserve to cover the potential demands of investors or depositors, they increase the amount of money in circulation. So the money in circulation is based on promissory notes, on debt. In order to further increase the amount of money in circulation, the Fed lowers the interest rate on its loans to banks to stimulate the economy, and in order to limit inflation it raises the interest rate.

Now the extraordinary thing is that the Federal Reserve Board is composed of representatives from the twelve Reserve Banks, and the Board's chairperson appointed by the President. So it is bankers who are the key players in setting the economic agenda of our nation, determining interest rates and the money supply of the US economy. They are, of course, interested in serving themselves, and in so doing they create an indebted society; think of credit cards, mortgages and of the student loan crisis.

That they serve their own interests and those who own capital is one of the reasons for growing income inequalities, as Thomas Piketty clearly shows in *Capital in the Twenty-First Century* (Harvard, 2014). The main driver of inequality is the historical tendency of capital to gain greater returns than the general rate of growth of the economy because of the underlying structures of political and economic power, including central banks. The role of the Fed in this unfair distribution of wealth was described in great detail by William Greider in *Secrets of the Temple: How the Federal Reserve Runs the Country* (Simon and Schuster, 1987), mentioned previously in Chapter 4 on the crisis of Western capitalism.

Understanding something about the nature of money and the different options we have in creating a medium of exchange that is not debt based is critical for our future. Some of the most important and interesting studies of money include, Ellen Brown, *Web of Debt* (Third Millenium Press, 5th edition, 2012); Stephen Zerlanga, *The Lost Science of Money* (American Monetary Institute, 2002); and Bernard Lietauer, *The Future of Money* (Random House, 2002). Also add Siegfried Finser, *Money Can Heal* (Steiner Books, 2006) for a discussion of gift, loan and purchase money; and Lynn Twist, *The Soul of Money* (W.W. Norton Co., 2003) for an exploration of the psychological and spiritual dimensions of money in our lives.

Potential solutions to the dilemma of debt money, created and controlled by the Federal Reserve, exist. The most direct is to have Congress simply take over the Federal Reserve since it is allowed to issue money by the Constitution, and indeed did so during the American Revolution and the Civil War. It would issue money as a measure of, and in accordance with, the level of economic activity, and would not charge interest but would spend this money into the economy, say with a large new infrastructure program or other agreed upon social needs. Since money is actually based on an agreement to accept wampum, coin, or printed dollars, as a medium of exchange this approach would work if there is sufficient political will. The American Monetary Institute has drafted a bill to this effect that could be introduced at a moment's notice. NESARA is a similar effort in giving Congress the authority to issue fiat currency, but it would be based on re-monetizing gold. We would go back to the gold standard which was abolished by Richard Nixon. (See http://www. nesara.us.pages/home.html for more information.)

Mutual Credit Associations such as the WIR network in Switzerland or LETS (Local Exchange Trading Systems) are examples of money as accounting systems that are successfully used in many parts of the world. Also, local complementary currencies such as Ithaca Dollars or Berkshares are a growing movement and a way to keep money in the regional economy. There is also the digital coin movement and the social credit system to consider. For a discussion of these and other options, go to www.commongoodbank and the work of John Root Jr, from whom I have gained a deeper understanding of money.

The second fundamental issue which needs re-thinking is the question of wages. I will describe the intolerable wage and wealth inequalities in the United States and other parts of the world in 'Toxic Excess' (Chapter 7), showing the impact of such inequalities on psychological and physical health, crime, police forces, and political and economic well-being. Given the facts of globalization and computerization it is quite clear that only between 15 and 30 per cent of people will have traditional forms of employment in the future, and most people will be self-employed or self-active. Some form of basic income will be required to maintain societal well-being, and multiple experiments are now underway in many parts of the world, all fiercely opposed by conservative groups who fear the liberating influence of not having to work for a living.

Recently, an article in the *Guardian* newspaper described a four-year experiment with a basic income, sufficient to cover basic needs, being awarded to every citizen in the town of Dauphin, outside of Winnipeg in Canada. The experiment was conducted in the mid-seventies but the resulting data has only been recently evaluated. It shows what could be predicted from the research of Richard Wilkinson and Kate Pickett in *The Spirit Level: Why Greater Equality Makes Societies Stronger* (Bloomsbury Press, 2010). People's health improved, educational achievement blossomed, poverty largely disappeared, and crime decreased. Lowering fear and anxiety has a salutary effect on body, soul and spirit.[1] What a surprise!

The third basic issue needing to be addressed is the economic and political power of large corporations. They have effectively escaped national control in the USA and Britain and in some other countries, lowering tax rates on income and profits, making society pay for many of the costs of pollution, environmental degradation, and community hardship, and have salted away profits in off-shore tax havens. International or global tax regulations are required, along with treating them as institutions, not persons. Citizens United needs to be overturned and political campaign contributions banned for all institutional entities. Lastly, corporate charter reform is essential to force all for-profit institutions to meet the criteria of profitability, community responsibility and environmental sustainability in the same way that non-profit organizations need to demonstrate that they are serving the public good in order to keep their non-profit status.

Lastly, we need to recognize that our social order is a human creation representing human thoughts and values, while at the same time it shapes our consciousness. If our society produces global poverty, suffering and ill health and violence as well as threatening our survival due to climate change, and it also produces egotism, fear and an ethos of the survival of the fittest, then it needs to be redesigned. There are many examples of what kind of social structures produce health and well-being for humans and indeed for all forms of life. It is this interplay of consciousness and social forms which is explored in the book of Otto Scharmer and Katrin Kaufer, *Leading from the Emerging Future: From Ego System to Eco System Economics*, (Berret-Koehler, 2013).

Rather than waiting for the large institutions of society to change and for a new money system to be inaugurated, we can take our money out of the large banks, participate in local investment networks and work toward a sustainable local economy such as Michael Shuman describes in *Local Dollars, Local Sense* (Chelsea Green, 2012).

Note

1   Rutger Bregman, 'Utopian thinking: the easy way to eradicate poverty', the *Guardian*, 5 March 2017.

Chapter 6

Common-Sense Outrage:
Move Your Money Now!
(April 2010)

Far more worrisome is the possibility that neither Washington nor Wall Street is willing to confront the deeper problem – the ascendancy of finance in national policy-making, (as well as in the gross domestic product), and the complicity of the politicians who really don't want to talk about it.

Kevin Phillips[1]

During my few recent conversations with people in the bank and investment houses of New York, I discovered that they are surprised that the American public is outraged at their behavior and their pay. I was astounded, as the outrage is common sense and completely justified, although the mainstream press and Wall Street bankers and traders seem to want to forget it, focusing instead on the few 'bad apples' in the industry, such as Bernie Madoff and R. Allen Stanford. The common-sense outrage says you, the bankers, took our money – savings, investments and retirement funds; then you used your political influence to decrease the regulation and capital reserve requirements of financial institutions so you could invest in and market mortgage-backed securities and credit default swaps, using our money to place risky investments from which you profited enormously. Then you pay yourselves huge bonuses, even after you helped to create the greatest global economic crisis since the late 1920s. Then, and this really tops it off, you turn to the Federal Government to use our tax dollars to bail you out of the mess you caused, while at the same time complaining about the regulation and restrictions which the government is seeking to impose on you.

This is truly astounding arrogance, for we, your customers, are paying you twice, having given you our private money to invest, which has lost about 40 per cent of its value since the stock-market high in the late winter of 2008; and then we pay you a second time through the huge government bail-out of the financial industry. People do get it; they have enough common sense to see a rip-off when they see one.

Many thoughtful observers would agree with Paul Krugman and Joseph Stiglitz, both Nobel prize winning economists, who argued for taking over the banking industry and breaking it up into smaller units so that none of them would be too 'big to fail again'. Instead, the government, under both Bush and Obama, has supported a further consolidation of the financial industry by, for example, pushing Merrill-Lynch into the arms of Bank of America, or insisting that Citi Group and Chase acquire smaller, insolvent banks.

So what can we, the easily manipulated but not unaware public, do? We can support the creation of a strong consumer protection agency for the financial industry presently being debated in Congress, as I write. We can also support stronger regulation of the financial instruments, including derivatives and short selling, raising capital reserve requirements and again separating commercial banks from investment houses. More importantly, we can bring a new consciousness to where we take our business, with whom we invest and bank, as many local banks, credit unions, and socially responsible investment funds did not participate in the sub-prime mortgage market. Smaller local banks, credit unions and co-operative banks have generally served the public well, taking deposits and providing loans to people in the community, the business of 'good money', as opposed to the 'questionable money' of speculative investment.

We can consider:

- Deciding which businesses and industries we want to support with our money.
- Placing our savings and investments with socially responsible investment funds, such as Domini, Calvert and Parnassus.
- Deposit our money with RSF Social Finance, the New Resource Bank in San Francisco, Triodos in Holland, the UK and Spain, and GLS in Bochum, Germany. All of them support farms, schools, therapy centers and sustainable businesses with their loan portfolios.

- Talking to our local banks and credit unions about their mission, ownership structure, loan and investment criteria, and then moving our accounts to them and away from the big multi-nationals.
- Supporting a local currency, as it keeps more money in the local area rather than being siphoned off to major urban centers or even abroad. In western Massachusetts, we have BerkShares that are accepted by most businesses as an alternative currency.
- Establishing a Local Investment Opportunity Network (LION on the web) which brokers a conversation between local initiatives in need of loans and investors who are looking for a better return than the half per cent or less being offered to depositors by the banks.

By taking such steps and avoiding Chase, Morgan Stanley, Citibank, Bank of America, Deutsche Bank, Wells Fargo, HBSC and other large international banks, we are using our common sense to avoid the worst offenders of the financial crisis and telling them that our disgust has consequences for their bottom line. We are also then connecting our money to our will, as opposed to simply placing it into an amorphous financial system that has little interest in serving genuine human needs.

Notes

1   Kevin Phillips, *Bad Money, Failed Politics and the Global Crisis of American Capitalism*, Penguin, New York, 2008, p. vii. For a review of relevant sources, a deeper analysis and proposals for reform, see 'The Crisis of Western Capitalism' (Chapter 4) and 'Reflections on the Global Economic Crisis and What to do About It' (Chapter 5) in this volume.

Chapter 7

Toxic Excess: Income Inequalities and the Fundamental Social Law
(October 2012)

We can have democracy in this country, or we can have great wealth concentrated in the hands of a few, but we cannot have both.

Louis Brandeis, Supreme Court Justice

The Effect of Income Inequalities in the United States

For many years I have been interested in the social ideas of Rudolf Steiner, sensing that if he was able to articulate such a deep and comprehensive imagination of child development as the basis for Waldorf education then surely what he had to say about the social issues of his time might also be important for us in the present. In addition to proposing a new threefold imagination of the social future as an answer to the devastation of the First World War, he formulated a set of social propositions which connect human consciousness and motives to social consequences. These laws are in most instances conditional, such as the Fundamental Social Law, which states,

> In a community of human beings working together, the well-being of the community (or region or country) is the greater, the less the individual claims for himself the proceeds of the work he has himself done; i.e. the more of those proceeds he makes over to his fellow workers, and the more his own requirements are satisfied, not out of his own work, but out of the work done by others.[1]

Steiner adds: 'every institution (or state and country) in a community of human beings that is contrary to this law will inevitably engender in some part of it, after some time, suffering and want.'[2]

The law points to the growth of egotism in wage-based economies in which every individual is encouraged to look out for their own interests at the expense of others, thereby producing long-term negative consequences. Steiner's law suggests that the question of motive for work is critical and that a competitive wage-based economy will enhance the egotism of the worker and that of society by creating the illusion that we essentially work for money rather than meaning or community well-being.

Laws are empirical propositions and can be tested. This I have attempted to do by exploring the physical, psychological, social, and economic effects of the competitive wage system in the United States based, as it is, on an unabashed neoliberal ideology, adhered to by both economic and political elites since the Reagan and Thatcher years. Neoliberalism views competition as the central characteristic of human relations and of society, and it suggests that the market is the final and best arbiter for labor, land and capital.

I was frankly shocked by the deep and profoundly negative human, psychological, economic and social impacts of income inequalities in the United States. In reviewing public health research and other studies, I found that growing income and wealth disparities in the United States since the late 1970s have decreased physical and mental health, increased prison populations and guard labor expenditures, decreased social mobility and opportunity, affected social trust and cohesion, undermined the fairness of the legal system, limited economic growth prospects and compromised democracy.

These conclusions, regarding the negative impact of large inequalities of wealth on the health and well-being of the USA and other societies, are increasingly shared by health researchers and social scientists at UNICEF and the United Nations Development Program (UNDP), as well as by many other social commentators. They were also popularized by the Occupy Movement in the United States, which made the large disparities of wealth and power between the 99 per cent and the 1 per cent a visible public cause in the autumn and winter of 2011. The research on income and wealth disparities unequivocally shows the truth of Martin Luther King's insight in his letter from a Birmingham Jail: 'All men are caught in an inescapable network of mutuality, tied in a single garment of destiny. Whatever affects one directly affects all indirectly.'[3] To put this slightly differently, we all suffer the consequences of stark differences in wealth and income.

The United States has the greatest wealth inequalities of any advanced Western society. The top 1 per cent controlled over 40 per cent of the nation's wealth, while the bottom 80 per cent only had 7 per cent in 2010; and more recent studies show that in 2012, the top one tenth of 1 per cent, led by over 400 family fortunes, controlled close to half of the nation's wealth. Such disparities have not been seen in the USA since 1929, during the Great Depression. According to revised census figures, the effective poverty rate in the USA was close to 16 per cent in 2014, with over 45 million people falling below the poverty line and spending over a third of their limited income on food.[4] In addition, the top 1 per cent of income earners took home 65 per cent of real income growth per family between 2002 and 2007, and it has become more extreme since then.[5] We have become a nation of 'Somebody's and Nobody's', to use Robert Fuller's apt phrase, with a frayed social safety net and growing social and economic hardship.[6] Little wonder that the Pew Foundation found in 2014 that 65 per cent of Americans view the government in a negative light, and banks and large corporations as untrustworthy and corrupt.

As a public health researcher noted, 'It isn't the absolute level of poverty that matters for population health as the size of the gap between rich and poor'. This gap negatively affects physical and mental health, drug abuse, education levels, imprisonment, obesity, violence, teen pregnancy and a host of other health risk factors.[7] The greater the gap between the wealthy and the poor, the worse the range of social, psychological and physical illness in society, as Wilkinson and Pickett and other health researchers have shown.[8] This is true for countries as well as the states and provinces of the USA and Canada.

The gap between the rich and the poor is also the primary cause of lowered longevity and increased disease in societies where per capita income levels are in excess of $5,000 per annum. The United States spends more than twice as much on health care as other countries of the OECD, yet ranks 48th in longevity, and does equally badly in many other health categories. Countries such as Japan, Sweden, Germany and Holland all perform considerably better. While the average spent per capita on health care in all of the OECD countries was $3,484 in 2014, it was in excess of $8,500 in the USA.[9] Given this difference in per capita health-care expenditures and outcomes, one would have thought that the health effects of income differentials would have played a significant role in the health-care reform debates held in the United States in 2009, as well as today. It has not – as both the mainstream media and politicians found it an inconvenient truth to deal with. More progressive taxation might have done more to improve health outcomes than changes in mandated healthcare, and might even be sufficient to pay for a single-payer system which all other Western nations have in one form or the other.

Prison Populations and Guard Labor

In addition to the psychological and physical health impact of wealth disparities, there is a second significant aspect to the impact of wealth disparities, viz. the greater the gap between the rich and the poor, the higher the prison population and the more a society spends on 'guard labor' – meaning defense, security and police. According to researchers at the Santa Fe Institute and the University of Massachusetts, there were more prison guards in the USA in 2012 than there were high school teachers.[10] The research draws a distinction between productive labor and guard labor; police, military personnel, and private security guards who all protect private property and maintain public order. Guard labor, while certainly an important part of total economic activity, is not productive in the same sense as producing goods and services for public consumption.

The United States, England and Greece have the highest percentage of guard labor in their total labor force of all Western countries, with almost one in four workers in the USA employed by the military, the police or security services. These countries also have some of the highest wealth and income disparities in Western societies.

According to the US Bureau of Justice statistics, there were over seven million people in the US prison system in 2009, or 3.1 per cent of the population – the highest per capita reported incarceration rate in the world. Indeed, with about 5 per cent of global population we had 23.5 per cent of the world's reported prison population at a cost of over $60 billion a year.[11] It is worthwhile noting that the number of Americans in prison grew rapidly after 1980, along with the cost of maintaining them, just as wealth inequalities were increasing during the years of the Reagan administration. The prison population in the USA increased until 2014, when it began to decline as a result of changes in the sentencing of drug offenders.

Our defense budget is of course much larger than that which is spent on prisons or security. In 2010 it is estimated that total defense expenditures exceeded $1 trillion when one factors in the wars in Afghanistan and Iraq.[12] While the defense budget decreased modestly in the second term of the Obama administration, it is still a huge percentage of total federal spending and, indeed, of our total GDP of over $14 trillion a year. In 2010 it was almost as much as the defense budgets of all other nations combined, and vastly in excess of what Russia and China spend together. Do we really need over 710 military bases in 80 countries, and to equip and maintain eleven aircraft carrier groups in all the oceans of the world?[13] Imagine the creative revolution that could occur if we devoted half of this, the people's money, to education, research, rebuilding the nation's infra-structure and alternative energy?

We have become both a Global Empire and a Garrison State, with extensive military personnel stationed abroad, as once the Roman legions were, and large prison populations and heavy security at home. What creates the fear and aggression which seems to characterize our society? Is it that we unconsciously recognize that we use a disproportionate amount of the world's resources to maintain our lifestyle choices and fear the poor and the dispossessed in our own communities because the growing gap between the rich and the poor seems both unfair and dangerous to us?

By fostering greater income equality through a more progressive tax system and cutting our military budget by 20 per cent we would save more than $4 trillion over the next ten years. By fostering greater equality of wealth we would strengthen the middle class, reduce health care and prison costs, increase domestic demand and have a healthier, more robust economy.

Economic Consequences

The economic argument about income inequalities is quite straight forward and, amazingly, is seldom discussed at this time of budget crises and limited growth. From 1945 until the mid 1970s the US economy flourished. As a result of the New Deal and the lessons learned from the Great Depression, there was a broad sense of social equity as progressive tax rates and wages increasing in line with productivity created the basis for a shared prosperity. Mariner Eccles, the Mid West banker and Chairman of the Federal Reserve, who more than anyone else helped pull the country out of the Depression in the 1930s, understood very clearly that great inequalities of wealth undermine economic prosperity, and that wealth and income needed to be shared more equitably if there was to be sufficient consumption to support an economic recovery.

After 1975 the economic and political insights resulting from the Great Depression were lost and working- and middle-class salaries began to diverge from increases in productivity. From 1980 to the present, median wages remained flat, when adjusted for inflation, and the government, from the Reagan years onward, pursued policies of privatization, deregulation and lowering tax rates on the wealthy and on corporations. Further consumption and economic growth was mainly achieved through women entering the work force in ever greater numbers, through the expansion of credit and through the granting of home equity loans. The resulting levels of indebtedness of families, corporations and the government were unsustainable when combined with the irresponsible and corrupt behavior of the financial sector and of regulatory agencies, and the Great Recession of 2008 occurred.

The lessons of the Depression of 1929 clearly need to be re-learned; great wealth disparities undermine demand, decrease consumption, increase unemployment and threaten to bankrupt the government and the nation. Robert Reich, the economist and social commentator, in his book *Aftershock: The Next Economy and America's Future*, argues persuasively that there will be no true economic recovery unless restoring greater equity in incomes becomes a national priority.[14]

Undermining Democracy

Increasing equality of incomes and opportunity would also go a long way toward restoring our democracy. Considering the Supreme Court decision in Citizens United in 2010, which allowed corporations to give unlimited amounts of money to political parties and candidates, and the wealth disparities in this country, we have an oligarchy of wealth and special interest groups controlling the political process. 'One dollar, one vote' has increasingly replaced 'one person, one vote'. The truth of this statement is reflected in the fact that large corporations and financial interests have managed to lower effective tax rates on wealthy Americans, to decrease both capital gains and corporate taxes and to get special government subsidies for select industries under both Republican and Democratic administrations. Meanwhile, our representatives managed to help eviscerate the unions and undermine the postwar social contract between American workers and their employers. With the expense of national political campaigns today and the rapid decline of union membership and finances, there is no other source of big money today than corporations and the wealthy. The saying 'Who pays the piper, calls the tune' was clearly described by Simon Johnson, the chief economist at the IMF from 2007–8, when he said some years ago: 'If the IMF's staff could speak freely about the U.S., it would tell us what it tells all countries in this situation: recovery will fail unless we break the financial oligarchy that is blocking essential reform.'[15]

I believe that we as Americans need to face up to the reality that we live in an oligarchy of wealthy economic and political elites, a plutocracy, well described by Joseph Stiglitz, the Nobel Prize winning economist, in an article titled 'Of the 1%, by the 1% and for the 1%'.[16] Stiglitz summarized his argument in his book, *The Price of Inequality: How Today's Divided Society Endangers our Future*,[17] by arguing that an economy and a society have been created in which great wealth is amassed through rent seeking, sometimes through direct transfers from the public to the wealthy, but more often through rules that allow the wealthy to collect 'rents' from the rest of society through monopoly power and other forms of exploitation.

The Fundamental Social Law and the Nature of Capitalism

It seems clear from the evidence cited that Steiner's insights into conditions of social health and illness are correct, and that an economy based on principles of market fundamentalism produces illness, suffering and want, not only in the United States but to some degree around the world. Following the Great Depression and the Second World War, an effort had been made to mitigate the negative effects of unvarnished capitalism through FDR's New Deal in the United States and extensive social welfare and labor legislation in the social democracies of Western Europe. These advances and the resulting amelioration of the worst aspects of capitalism have been systematically undermined in the USA and Great Britain since the late 1970s. Buttressed by the 'efficient market orientation' of the Chicago School of Economics, the Republican Right in the USA and the Conservatives in Britain have promoted a neoliberal economic ideology which one *Guardian* observer described as being 'at the root of all our problems'. In describing this ideology, he notes:

> ...regulation should be minimized, public services should be privatized. The organization of labour and collective bargaining by trade unions are portrayed as market distortions that impede the formation of a natural hierarchy of winners and losers. Inequality is recast as virtuous: a reward for utility and a generator of wealth, which trickles down to enrich everyone. Efforts to create a more equal society are both

counterproductive and morally corrosive. The market ensures that everyone gets what they deserve.[18]

The central values and core principles lying behind neoliberalism were well summarized by David Korten when he stated:

1   People are primarily motivated by self-interest, as expressed through the quest for financial gain and power.
2   The actions which are taken by individuals and groups to maximize their financial gain and influence bring the greatest benefit to society.
3   Social and economic life is primarily characterized by competition, rather than cooperation, by the struggle for existence, and society is best organized around this principle.
4   Human progress should be measured by the consumption and production of goods and services as expressed by the Gross Domestic Product (GDP).[19]

This is Social Darwinism all over again; the poor deserve their suffering and the rich merit their hard-earned wealth. The fact that corporations and economic elites have 'captured' Washington, London and other capitals as well as state and local governments is conveniently ignored. The need for rethinking the social contract and, indeed, the nature and structure of society is quite clear, if we are to avoid the worst aspects of an authoritarian oligopoly.

Increasing equality of incomes and wealth is therefore not only a moral imperative but also an essential strategy for improving the health and well-being of societies. Before looking at some possible solutions to the scourge of high levels of income and wealth disparities, let me note that in no way do I want to ignore or deny the even greater injustices and inequalities which exist between the wealthy, more industrial and post-industrial societies of the world and those countries in Africa, South America and Asia who struggle with widespread famine, great poverty and violence. When 1 per cent of the earth's population owns over 40 per cent of the globe's wealth, as they also do in the USA, and over 40,000 people – mainly children – die of starvation every day, the balance between wealthy and poor nations is clearly of greater import, and should be of greater social concern than the growing wealth disparities in the United States itself.

Fixing the Existing System: Taxes and Financial Regulation

If we accept the basic tenets of capitalism, there is much that can be done to promote greater equality of income and wealth through more progressive tax rates and other measures. A study carried out by the *New York Times* in November 2012 found that tax rates had declined substantially for most Americans, except the poor, between 1980 (during the Reagan years) and the present day. Not only have income taxes declined, but so have capital gains taxes, a primary vehicle for the wealthy to increase their fortunes, and corporate and estate taxes. In 2000, for example, 94 per cent of all US firms paid taxes of less than 5 per cent on their profits.[20]

Increasing top income-tax rates, raising the capital gains taxes from 15 per cent to 25 or 30 per cent and lowering the estate tax exemptions from the present levels of $6 million to $1 million, would do a great deal to balance the budget of the federal government, as well as producing a more equitable and healthier society. The closing of tax loopholes for businesses, increasing the effective corporate tax, as well as shutting down off-shore tax shelters would also restore more equity to the system.

Joseph Stiglitz also points to the need to fix the financial system, including improved regulation, restoring competition to the banking sector, improving corporate governance and transparency, as well as a comprehensive reform of the bankruptcy laws.[21] He mentions other steps as also being essential to creating a healthier and more equal society, such as improving access to medical care through a single-payer system, providing equal access to higher education, and strengthening government programs such as Social Security, Medicaid, Food Stamps and unemployment assistance. In asking the question of whether there is a genuine hope for reform of this kind, he suggests that there are two interconnected developments that could offer the possibility of transformation. One is that the 99 per cent of the population realizes that they have been duped, or 'sold a bill of goods', by the 1 per cent and become politically active, as happened in the Middle East during the Arab Spring. The other is that the 1 per cent realizes that it is actually in their interest politically and economically to work toward a more equitable society. Yet as Stiglitz and other observers recognize, without a reform of the political system and the public financing of elections, changes within American society are likely to be stalemated by the influence of private and corporate funds. It is as Justice Brandeis stated almost a century ago: great inequalities of wealth and true democracy are not compatible.

Improved Wages and a Guaranteed Basic Income

A more far-reaching set of solutions could be found by asking questions about the nature of work and remuneration. If work and an adequate standard for living are seen as a right, such as is articulated in the UN Universal Declaration of Human Rights and President Roosevelt's Economic Bill of Rights, then quite different a venues o f r eform a re possible.

There is a ladder of steps that could be taken to move toward a living wage as a human right. The most basic is to raise the minimum wage. Presently, the federal minimum wage in the USA is $7.25 an hour, a decrease of over 30 per cent since 1979 when adjusted for inflation. Substantially raising the minimum wage, as some municipalities and states have done, would to some degree help reduce inequality.

A more fundamental step is articulated by the Living Wage Movement, which is to establish a floor of what is required to live at a basic level in different regions of the country. Th e Ii ving Wa ge Mo vement has successfully conducted campaigns to raise wages in selected cities, such as Santa Fe and New York City, and is attempting to develop state-wide and national campaigns. It has found that the argument of economic justice, viz. that a full-time worker should be able to live and support him- or herself and some dependents on the wages earned, has found substantial resonance among American voters, many of whom have at some point in their life worked for the minimum wage.

In 1969 President Nixon, influenced by Daniel Patrick Moynihan, considered the question of welfare reform, and proposed a Family Assistance Plan of direct payments to families with children, in part arguing that a basic living should be a right. While this plan did not pass in Congress because of amendments to the proposed legislation, it did set a precedent that Republicans, or the political right, could be persuaded that there are alternatives to welfare reform which move in the direction of a guaranteed income.

A Guaranteed Basic Income, or Citizen's Income, is a well-developed movement in many parts of the world, and is articulated by an international organization called the Basic Income Network. It is an idea that was expressed by Martin Luther King in his last book before being assassinated, *Where Do We Go from Here – Chaos or Community?*, and has the support of many Nobel Prize winning economists from both the left and the right of the political spectrum, including Herbert Simon, Friedrich Hayek, James Meade, Robert Solow and Milton Friedman.[22]

The concept is quite simple. Every citizen is paid a basic stipend from birth, irrespective of need. Such a stipend is seen as a right, and is financed either out of the revenues of State enterprises or State leasing revenue, such as is paid by the State of Alaska to all of its citizens; or it is funded by a sales or value-added tax which many European countries already have in place.

There are many virtues to the Guaranteed Basic Income, one of which is recognizing that work is by no means limited to paid employment when we consider the variety of human activity, from raising children to the care of the elderly, artistic activities, gardening or spending time and energy to volunteer for an environmental or social cause. Another is recognizing that developed and highly specialized and computerized economies do not need to employ more than 20 per cent of the population in order to create the surpluses needed to support a society, as Jeremy Rifkin and others have argued.[23] An additional benefit would be to lead individuals and societies to recognize that individuals do not work mainly for money, above a certain basic level, but for meaning, contact and value, as numerous studies have shown.[24] These studies make a very convincing case that it is the challenge, contact and meaning of work which provide the real motive for labor in all of its many forms. A Guaranteed Basic Income would, in addition, rid us of the often-demeaning and highly bureaucratic welfare system.

Providing a basic income would also lead us in the direction of seeing an adequate standard of living as a right, i.e. as a rights question more than an economic question, for which Rudolf Steiner already argued almost a century ago. It would certainly enhance creativity and right livelihood, as people would be drawn to those activities which give satisfaction, meaning and joy. Coupling a Basic Income with universal healthcare, progressive taxation and free education would go a long way toward reducing income inequality and poverty, and create much more dynamic and healthier societies. This was shown to be the result of a four-year experiment with a Basic Income in Dauphin, Canada. Between 1974 and 1978, people received a stipend which allowed everyone to have sufficient income to cover basic living costs. Health improved and hospital visits decreased, children did better at school, there was less domestic violence and juvenile delinquency, people did not quit their jobs, and the local economy prospered.[25]

Perhaps the planned basic-income experiments in Finland, Scotland, Germany and Switzerland will have similar results. Why should we be surprised that when people struggle to survive, or to have safe housing and enough to eat, that they become psychologically and physically ill, especially when living in societies that shame them by constantly promoting the images and products of the rich? Abraham Maslow, Rudolf Steiner and Martin Luther King were quite right: mutual aid and support is a far better foundation for a healthy society and healthy people than an economy and society committed to a competitive struggle for survival. The research is there to support a different society; what we lack is the imagination and the political will.

Notes

1   Rudolf Steiner, *Anthroposophy and the Social Question*, Steiner Press, Great Barrington, Mass., 2004.
2   Ibid., p. 34.
3   Martin Luther King, 'Letter from a Birmingham Jail', reprinted in *The Atlantic*, April 2013.
4   Emmanuel Saez, 'The evolution of top incomes in the U.S.', pdf elsa. Berkley.edu. Also quoted in Max Ehrenfried, 'Democrats internal dispute about the white working class is about to get real', *Washington Post*, 10 July 2017.
5   Saez, ibid.
6   Robert Fuller, *Somebody's and Nobody's: Overcoming the Abuse of Rankism*, New Society Publishers, 2003.
7   Peter Montague, 'Economic Inequality and Health', Environmental Research Foundation, Report No. 437; pdf.elsa.berkeley.edu.
8   R. Wilkinson and K. Pickett, *The Spirit Level: Why Greater Equality Makes Societies Stronger*, Bloomsbury Press, New York, 2009, in particular pp. 49–173. Also, Stephen Bezrucha, 'Is globalization bad for our health?', *Western Journal of Medicine*, 172 (May), 2000, pp. 332–334.
9   OECD Health Statistics, 2010–2017.
10   Samuel Bowles and Arjun Jayadev, 'Garrison America', Economist's Voice, The Berkeley Electronic, March 2007
11   Wikipedia: U.S. Prison Populations.
12   Robert Dreyfuss, 'Taking aim at the Pentagon budget', *The Nation*, 11 April 2011.
13   See the excellent book by Chalmers Johnson, *The Sorrows of Empire: Militarism, Secrecy and the End of the Republic*, Metropolitan Books, New York, 2004, in particular pp. 32–56 for a description of American military commitments around the globe.
14   See Robert B. Reich, *Aftershock: The Next Economy and America's Future*, Alfred Knopf, New York, 2010, pp. 28–38. See also the insightful and colorful book by Kevin Phillips, *Wealth and Democracy*, Broadway Books, New York, 2002.
15   Simon Johnson, 'The quiet coup', *The Atlantic*, May 2009.
16   Joseph Stiglitz, 'Inequality: Of the 1%, by the 1% and for the 1%', *Vanity Fair*, May 2011; available online at goo.gl/3h42Qz (accessed 30 March 2019).
17   Stiglitz, *The Price of Inequality: How Today's Divided Society Endangers our Future*, W.W. Norton, New York, 2012, p. 266.
18   George Monbiot, 'Neoliberalism: The ideology at the root of all our problems', The *Guardian*, 15 April 2016.
19   David Korten, *When Corporations Rule the World*, Berrett-Koehler, San Francisco, 1995, pp. 70–71.

20   'Complaints aside, most face lower tax burdens than in the Reagan 80's', *New York Times*, 30 November 2012.
21   Stiglitz, op. cit., pp. 264–284.
22   Wikipedia, 'Basic Income'.
23   Jeremy Rifkin, *The End of Work: The Decline of the Global Labor Force and the Dawn of the Post Market Era*, Putnam, New York, 1995.
24   Daniel Pink, *Drive: The Surprising Truth About What Motivates Us*, Penguin, New York, 2009.
25   Rutger Bregman, 'Utopian thinking: the easy way to eradicate poverty', The *Guardian*, 6 March 2016.

Part IV:

Looking for Hope in Difficult Times

Chapter 8

Navigating Chaos in the Age of Trump:
A Call for Discernment
(15 February 2017)

Always the assumption is that we can first set demons at large and then, somehow, become smart enough to control them.

Wendell Berry[1]

Donald Trump's Reality TV Show has moved to the White House. He now has a global audience. Early morning tweets, ill-considered executive orders, personal insults to judges and foreign leaders who disagree with him, and insistence on the truth of easily discredited lies – all create an explosive, consciousness-draining toxic media environment. Whilst even his admirers acknowledge his hypersensitivity to criticism, his aggressiveness, ignorance of the issues and his inability to confess error, we all continue to attend to him, and diminish ourselves, by hanging on his every word.[2]

Trump supporters feel that he is really doing what, during the campaign, he said he would, while the rest of us cannot believe he is putting a ban on Muslims from seven countries, planning to build a wall at the Mexican border, currying favor with Putin's Russia, and deporting immigrants in record numbers.

Remarkably, given his quixotic nature, Trump has been quite consistent in his statements, beliefs and actions from the start of the presidential campaign through his (as I write) current four-week old presidency. He has promised to put America first, to alter or cancel unfavorable or ineffective trade deals, to force American companies to keep or bring jobs home, to strengthen the military, and to weaken governmental regulation, especially in regard to energy and the environment. He will also vigorously pursue the War against Terror, limit immigration from Mexico and most Latin countries, and halt it entirely from many Muslim countries. Trump has also aligned himself with most of the traditional goals of the Republican party and its evangelical Christian base. He doubts climate change, and plans to withdraw the USA from climate change agreements, while also cancelling many EPA goals and guidelines. He supports overturning Obamacare, de-funding Planned Parenthood, weakening LGBT rights, and improving decaying US infrastructure; and he plans to appoint one or more conservative Supreme Court Justices.

For a person concerned about human rights, race relations, peace prospects and the environment, this frightening agenda is made worse by Trump's actual and planned Cabinet appointments, which consist primarily of older white men from the conservative wing of the Military Industrial Complex. With his appointments, Medicare and Social Security are at risk, public lands will be sold to private interests, Wall Street again has its fingers in the pot of the Treasury Department, agricultural interests will have a field day through an industrial agriculture champion in Sonny Purdue, and public education can be stripped of resources by Betsy de Vos of the Amway fortune.

This is the country's wealthiest cabinet in history, and an administration that makes a mockery of separating private financial interests from public goals and actions. The Trump Presidency makes fully visible to all American citizens, and indeed to the world, the truth of the old adage that what is good for General Motors is good for America: it cements corporate influence and control over both American government and much of American culture.

Basic Concerns

When I subdue my outrage at the new administration and its goals and think more deeply, I have to acknowledge a set of quite basic existential, human and moral concerns. The first of these has already been alluded to, viz. that the Trump Presidency Reality TV Show is absorbing a great deal of the world's attention and consciousness. This means that millions of people's psychic and spiritual energy is fearfully focused on him. Does this give him greater power and the ability to unduly influence the psyche of humanity? I certainly think so, and know that his many threats and ongoing lies enhance the distraction, unease and fear living in my soul and that of many others. So we all need to learn to disinfect ourselves daily, to clean our souls of 'Trump*itis*', by not rushing to the media to see the latest insult or outrage, and by learning to look with quietness and discernment at what is transpiring in Washington, D.C. and around the world. Otherwise, Trump blocks our creativity and insight, sows confusion in our soul, and lames our will for doing the good.

A second concern has to do with undermining the truth, through the outright lying and the creation of 'alternative facts' by Trump and the spokespeople of his administration. If he can persuade enough people that there are conservative facts and liberal facts, one no better than the other, then civilization is lost, because the possibility of dialogue, of distinction between facts and interpretations, is gone, and objective science and knowledge denied. As a recent columnist noted, the effort to negate truth, to discredit the press and to call into question scientific university research 'poisons the well of democratic discourse'.[3]

The Trump Presidency also represents a threat to our constitution and to our democracy; and to not acknowledge this is to be blind to a danger that many Germans denied in the 1930s, to their later dismay. As Hannah Arendt, the political thinker and authority on totalitarian regimes, noted, a culture of fear, the militarization of society, the abridgement of human rights, the undermining of independent courts – all are characteristics of authoritarian, totalitarian regimes. So is the stifling of dissent, the curtailment of a free press, the demonization of the other, the attack on the rights of labor, and the glorification of the nation.[4] Trump and his administration unfortunately manifest these tendencies to a marked degree, leading me to question all efforts to accommodate or normalize relationships with the present administration or the Republican Congress which supports it.

Underlying these concerns is the worry about the stability, health and maturity of Trump's personality. When I watch and listen to him, I get the impression of an extremely wounded, insecure bully who always has to be the biggest, the best, the wealthiest, the most handsome – an all around winner who can never admit weakness, and who has to attack anyone who challenges him.

In addition to the worry about the authoritarian tendencies of the administration, I fear the threat to world peace posed by our new chief executive. How easy it is to move from a war of words to acts of war when the White House is occupied by an insecure, psychologically challenged person, supported by advisors such as Stephen Bannon and Stephen Miller, acknowledged provocateurs, or 'bomb throwers', from the conspiracy-laden alt-right movement.

I also have a concern about whether the divisive nature of the election will play itself out in an actual impeachment process, for which calls are already being made on the internet, possibly leading to a military take-over of our government by a threatened Trump Presidency. If Bill Clinton can be subjected to impeachment proceedings by lying about an affair with a White House intern, then the Trump White House is infinitely more vulnerable, with its hidden relations with Putin's Russia and its many conflicts of interest, crony capitalism and sleazy deals.

The taint of the Trump Presidency being illegitimate is already quite strong, with James Comey, the director of the FBI, illegally announcing a renewed investigation of Clinton's e-mail server eleven days before the election, and Russian intelligence operatives attempting to influence the election through releasing strategic leaks and fake news. The recent forced resignation of General Flynn and the inappropriate, if not illegal, contacts between the Trump campaign and the Russian leadership further undermine the legitimacy of the Trump Presidency.[5] In addition, people are aware that Republicans deleted thousands of inner-city residents, as well as Latinos and Asians, from the voting rolls in North Carolina, Ohio, Pennsylvania and Michigan through |Operation Crosscheck, a computer program which deletes voters from rolls when duplicate or similar names appear in other states, but often without comparing social security numbers or middle initials.[6] If this becomes front-page news, beware the backlash of angry liberals who already feel that two elections were stolen from them.

Many Americans remember the strange election of George W. Bush in 2000, when a conservative Supreme Court blocked a recount in Florida which, according to knowledgeable observers, would have given Gore enough votes to swing the election, as over 50,000 African American voters had been removed from voter rolls in Dade County. As it was, Gore won the popular vote, and so did Hilary Clinton, by close to three million votes, in the recent election. Perhaps as one observer noted, we need to add 11/09 (i.e. the election result) to 9/11 as an important marker in our history. The call for 'regime change', which the War on Terror unleashed in other countries 15 years ago, has now come home to haunt us in a media-manipulated and fear-based election.[7] I was surprised by the Democratic party's quiet and quick acquiescence to the election results in both cases.

If this election is a harbinger of what we have to face as citizens of a 'democratic society' in the future, then I fear for our children and grandchildren. Fake news and the marketing of lies, the existence of the omnipresent national security state monitoring our daily communications, the promotion of fear and aggressive nationalism, and the selling of empty personalities as leaders through specialized, personalized Facebook programs and other social media – all this evokes what Trump ally and former Fox chairman Roger Ailes already stated in 1968: 'This is a whole new concept. This is it. This is the way they will be elected for ever more. The next guys will have to be performers.'[8] And so a populace which watches television an average of five hours a day, or 39 hours a week, and in addition spends many hours on the internet, elects a reality show TV star to become president, confirming that our national political reality reflects the dynamics and false images created by the media. It is as philosopher and social critic Jean Baudrillard predicted: in the post-modern age, the representation, the simulacrum, precedes, shapes and now determines (political) reality.[9]

Inner and Outer Discernment

So what is it that we can do as concerned Americans and citizens of a world in crisis? Clearly, we can be politically and socially active in many domains, from protesting to political organizing to running for local office. The liberal media is full of specific and often insightful recommendations on what can be done to resist, including Michael Moore's ten actions that will limit the power of the Trump Presidency.[10] Moreover, in our towns and neighborhoods there are many inspiring initiatives and leaders who are busy improving our communities, as Sarah van Gelder describes in her new book, *The Revolution where You Live*, and we can join and support such efforts.[11]

But there is much we can and need to do at an inner level, too. One thing is to monitor our soul state, to avoid the excesses of withdrawal and disengagement, or of hyperactivity and possible violence. In the one instance, we retreat into our private world of favorite pastimes, or we contemplate moving to New Zealand, or we descend into brooding and depression. With the other, the danger is to be so outraged and obsessed that we feverishly engage in every possible demonstration and activity and are haunted by the constant stream of bad news. With either of these extremes we risk losing ourselves and our equilibrium, just what our lesser selves and the negative working forces in the world are wanting, as described in the essay, 'Witnessing the Long Emergency' (Chapter 1, this volume).[12]

Can we, instead, practice being active witnesses to that which lives in our soul and to that which lives in the world? To do so means creating moments of inner and outer quiet, taking time out from the busy stream of our lives to sit, to reflect, to engage in mindfulness activities, and to pray or meditate for guidance and insight in order to serve that which is good, that which is life enhancing in the world. And if we feel down-caste or fearful, we can remember Thich Nhat Hanh's advice, 'Around us life bursts forth with miracles – a glass of water, a ray of sunshine, a leaf, a caterpillar, a flower, laughter'.[13] Or, 'we can discover that in reality no single day passes without a miracle happening in our life', as Rudolf Steiner suggested.[14] And then we can note what Rebecca Solnit wisely adds: '… when you face a politics that aspires to make you fearful, alienated, and isolated, joy is a fine initial act of resurrection'.[15]

When we take the time to quiet down, to stop the incessant chattering that goes on in our mind, we can also come to an experience that 'a sense for truth is the silent language of the soul'.[16] Whether we are pondering a question of our life's direction, or of a relationship or of politics and economics, if we remove the external admonition that it is all too complex for us to understand anyway, or that the experts say this or that, and instead rely on our own common sense, we can come to our own sound judgements. If we give an issue or a question time, it will reveal its truth to us because in the quiet of our soul, there is a sense for truth, for fairness, for community, and for life. We need to allow it to speak.

If we cannot really trust government to speak the truth, and we know that many professions have been captured by corporate interests, and that the media is invariably biased in one direction or the other, we must learn to rely on our own, hopefully informed judgement, on our soul wisdom. I knew instinctively that the second invasion of Iraq was based on a lie, despite the support for the invasion provided by the *New York Times*. I felt my stomach turn, and I became very uneasy about the coming election the moment Comey said he was renewing Clinton's e-mail server investigation. I also do know when I have told a lie, or have not done my best for a client or a friend, even though I may try hard to block such an awareness. A sense for truth becomes the language of the soul only if we give it the time and attention to shape our thoughts, feelings and actions. And it will speak in diverse ways, sometimes as a feeling or a thought, and sometimes from the outside through a song, an article or a chance comment from a stranger. We need to practice listening to it, and to give it our attention, for I believe it is our essential being that is then speaking in our soul, helping us to a deeper discernment.

Our View of Good and Evil

We cannot avoid the need to make moral judgements about ourselves and the world. The source of such judgements and our conceptions of good and evil are nurtured in our childhood, in our upbringing and education. The question is whether our criteria of judgement are conscious or can be made conscious, or whether our judgements are so automatic that they have captured us. It is an important exercise to write down on what basis we judge something or someone to be good, helpful, moral or its opposite, and how it is that we sense these qualities to be present or not. The age we live in and the recent election give us ample opportunity to practice such awareness.

Recently I went to a documentary film titled 'I Am Not Your Negro' about James Baldwin, the black writer and activist. It is a searing look at the civil-rights era and the struggle for justice by Black Americans from the time of slavery to the present day. While I was watching it and the scenes of white prejudice and violence, I thought that many Americans would find this intolerable to watch, and would seek to deny our terrible history toward 'the other', toward indigenous peoples, African Americans, Asians, Latinos, refugees and immigrants. And perhaps I could only watch it, but with dismay, because I have been blessed with mixed-race grandchildren, or remember being a young immigrant of seven and being told to go back home by a group of playground bullies.

Before I provide a brief list of my own criteria, and ask you to create your own, I want to express my deep conviction that we are each capable of the greatest crimes, and the most sublime love and kindness. Under certain conditions I can imagine myself as a thief, a murderer, a tyrant and a criminal. I can find many instances in my life of behavior that I regret, and find its sources in fear and egotism. I also have no trouble in locating the Trump in me, from vanity about my hair, to lying in order to get my way, to deeply resenting criticism from others, even when I know it is well deserved.

The distinctions I make between good and evil are based on asking what is life enhancing, joy creating, community building, love engendering, diversity strengthening, nature honoring and gratitude based, and what is not. Egotism, selfishness, race baiting, misogyny, profiteering, not honoring the truth or agreements, fostering violence and greed, denying the human spirit and the possibility of love and kindness are, to my mind, regressive, patriarchal, unbalanced and evil. I think that many of our institutions in Western society, which foster blind consumption, ecological recklessness, human exploitation and selfish greed, are manifestations of structural evil, as Cynthia Moe-Lobeda calls it; that is, they are based on assumptions, and produce outcomes which are life threatening.[17]

The reality and truth of structural evil in our society are concisely described by Mahatma Gandhi in his summary of Seven Deadly Social Sins:

- Wealth without Work (the rent-seeking culture of our investment and business world described by Robert Stiglitz and others)
- Pleasure without Conscience
- Knowledge without Character (knowledge that is manipulative and control oriented)
- Commerce without Morality
- Science without Humanity
- Religion without Sacrifice
- Politics without Principle

Gandhi first published this description in 1926, and then handed it, written on a scrap of paper, to his grandson the day before he was assassinated.[18] It is still an apt description of much of what ails us as a society, and it contains explicit moral judgements which we are not comfortable making in a predominately secular and materialistic society. Yet I believe modern life and the many crises we face will force us to come to grips with questions of good and evil to an ever-greater extent, as we will not be able to discern the false prophets of our time without such a matrix of judgement.

Crucial in making such moral judgements is distinguishing the policy, statement or position from the individual espousing it. We can say that a blanket policy of deporting immigrants has evil consequences, or that the indiscriminate use of fossil-fuel extraction is evil, given what we know about climate change, but we should not demonize the individuals who hold such views. The truth of this was brought home to me recently in talking to a family member who is a Trump supporter, but who as a person goes out of his way to help people in trouble, even financially. He has a generosity of heart that often humbles me, and for which I have great respect, even-though I struggle greatly to understand his political and social beliefs.

Subtle Activism: Connecting the Inner and Outer World

There are two powerful but incorrect messages which the modern world intones. The first is that you as an individual have no influence and no power unless you are wealthy, control an organization, have a TV show, or are part of a larger mass movement. The second is based on the Cartesian separation of mind and matter: what is significant is what is observable in the physical world – behavior matters but not your thoughts and feelings.

Both are manifestly incorrect. It is only individuals who, together with others, bring about change in the world. It is individual women and men who heard about the ban on immigrants and rushed to the airports to offer their legal or translation services. It is individuals who protest war, corruption and racial violence, and who conceive of and create alternative technologies and social innovations.

Modern scientific research 'is increasingly coming to embrace the notion that consciousness and world, or mind and matter, are complexly interrelated'.[19] We know that meditation and prayer can help friends to heal or recover from illness, that observer and observed are linked in intangible ways, and that plants will react to aggressive or peaceful thoughts. And we know that the social world – the world of families, towns, schools, roads, violence, friendships and conversations – is supported and made possible by a rich web of understandings, concepts and feelings. So we can say that we live in one world, in which outer and inner are deeply interconnected.

Some years ago a friend wrote a small book with the title *Nothing to Do with Me*, suggesting that all social issues have an inner side which, when we identify them, allows us to work for healing and transformation in both an inner and an outer way. He cites the case of political torture, and suggests that it is based on not seeing the humanity of the other, and then wonders what we are doing to the store clerk or the toll collector when we do not acknowledge or look at him or her.[20] What would happen to the psychological and spiritual balance of forces in the world if ever-more people made a practice of looking into the eyes of the other, acknowledging their humanity, and inwardly or outwardly thanking them for their help.

If we are upset by how immigrants are treated, also an instance of objectifying, or by othering them, what happens when we make it a practice to speak to people in our lives who are foreign, and offering them friendship and human support in times of need. If we are bothered by the crony capitalism of the Trump administration or the constant lying, how do we deal with truth and lying in ourselves, and how is it that we make financial agreements with others who work for us? Are we fair in what we pay and what we expect, and do we have transparent conversations about such matters? There are a host of such practices we can begin which, I believe, affect the balance of good and evil in the world, and which counter the egotism, conceit, corruption and manipulation of our times. Practicing just a few will serve to make us feel less helpless, and will serve the good in the world each day.

Notes

1   Wendell Berry, *Standing by Words: Essays*, North Point Press, San Francisco, 1983, p. 65.
2   *LA Times*, Vol. 16, Issue 791.
3   Lawrence Douglas, 'Why Trump wants to disempower institutions that protect the truth', The *Guardian*, 7 February 2017.
4   See Henry Giroux, 'Normalizing Trump's authoritarianism is not an option', *Tikun*, 19 January 2017.
5   Julian Berger, 'Flynn's resignation likely not the beginning of Trump's Russia Woes – nor the end', The *Guardian*, 14 February 2017.
6   Greg Palast, 'The GOP's stealth war against voters', *Rolling Stone*, 24 August 2016.
7   Tom Engelhard, 'Was 11/8 a New 9/11?', *RSN*, 2 December 2016.
8   Cited in Douglas Kellner, *Television and the Crisis of Democracy*, Westview Press, Los Angeles, 1990, p. 65.
9   In his book *Simulacra and Simulation*, Jean Baudrillard (English translation, 1994) makes the argument that post-modern society is shaped, and to some degree determined, by television and the electronic media.
10 Michael Moore, 'Do these ten things and Trump will be toast', *RSN*, 22 February 2017.
11 Sarah van Gelder, *The Revolution Where You Live*, Berrett-Koehler, San Francisco, 2017. See also her edited book, *Sustainable Happiness: Live Simply, Live Well, Make a Difference*, Berrett-Koehler, San Francisco, 2014.
12 See Tom Atlee, *Random Communications from an Evolutionary Edge*, Essay: 'Our responses to evolutionary threats'.
13 Thich Nhat Hanh, *Your True Home*, #3, Shambala Publications, Boulder, Colo., 2011.
14 Rudolf Steiner, *The Work of the Angels in Man's Astral Body*, Rudolf Steiner Press, London, 1972, p. 37,
15 Rebecca Solnit, *Hope in the Dark: Untold Histories, Wild Possibilities*, Haymarket Books, Chicago, Ill., 2016, p. 24.
16 Rudolf Steiner, *Staying Connected*, Steiner Books, Great Barrington, Mass., 2009, p. 38.
17 Cynthia Moe-Lobeda, *Resisting Structural Evil: Love as Ecological-Economic Vocation*, Fortress Press, Minneapolis, Minn., 2013, pp. 3–4.
18 M. Gandhi, *The Seven Deadly Social Sins*; see original plus commentary at http://www.gandhiinstitute.org.
19 David Nicol, *Subtle Activism: The Inner Dimension of Social and Planetary Transformation*, State University of New York Press, Albany, NY, 2012, pp. 1–16.
20 Alexander Bos, *Nothing to Do with Me*, Floris Books, Edinburgh, 2004; available from Stichting Dialoog, Holland.

Chapter 9

Looking for Hope in Difficult Times
(December 2017)

What we dream of is already present in the world.

Rebecca Solnit

What is the Nature of Hope?

Recently while watching some episodes of Ken Burn's and Lynn Novick's *The Vietnam War*, I heard the Peter, Paul and Mary song, 'Where Have All the Flowers Gone?' and the fitting refrain, 'when will they ever learn…'. The United States continues to be at war in Afghanistan and Iraq, we are still supporting corrupt foreign regimes, we are again using our airpower to take the lives of innocent civilians, and we continue losing American lives, with no end in sight and no clear rationale for our military involvement in the Middle East, Africa or elsewhere.

Being immersed in images and memories of the Vietnam War, and the growing resistance to it, put me in a melancholy frame of mind, and made me remember the many lies of four administrations about the invasion of Vietnam, as well as the repeated assurances of military commanders that victory was just a few months away. What has changed, I ask myself? The same lack of honesty can be found in debates about gun control, climate change, income inequalities and the police killings of inner-city residents. And yet, somehow, I still have a hope that we as a people and a country can learn to hearken to truth, can develop more compassion, can deepen our democracy, and will share the benefits of our economic prosperity more widely, despite so much evidence to the contrary.

As I ponder why I am still positive about our society's and humanity's prospects, why I still have hope, I am reminded of Vaclav Havel's words, while suffering under a repressive communist regime in Czechoslovakia in the mid 1980s:

> Either we have hope in us or we don't. It is a dimension of the soul.... Hope is not prognostication. It is an orientation of the Spirit, an orientation of the heart; it transcends the world that is immediately experienced, and is anchored somewhere beyond its horizons.[1]

I think such a hopeful orientation of the heart rests on an awareness of the long-term positive direction of human and societal development, of the movement toward greater inner and outer freedom. As Martin Luther King noted many years ago during a sermon at Wesleyan University, 'the arc of the moral universe is long, but it bends towards justice'.[2] We have ended slavery in most parts of the world. While the struggle for women and gay rights continues unabated, and prejudice, racism, misogyny and fear of the other are still very much alive in all parts of the world, enormous progress has been made against the three great traditional scourges of humanity; starvation, plague and war. Periodic starvation killed millions of people in Europe, Africa and Asia as late as the nineteenth century, and in China and Africa during the twentieth. The Black Death in the fifteenth century led to the death of between a quarter and a third of the populations of the great European cities, and the Spanish flu in the early twentieth century killed more people than died in the hostilities of the First World War. Death by disease and plague has decreased dramatically, and has been contained and managed in the last decades – witness the efforts with Ebola in Africa, or the Avian flu in Asia.

War has also been with us since our earliest beginnings, and while it continues in awful ways, more people died of suicide in the last decade than as a result of armed conflict and terrorism.[3]

Such a broad view of progress in human evolution can also be married to a more detailed perspective on what is going well now, of where real progress is taking place around the world, and in our own communities. For example, extreme poverty, defined as living on less than $2 a day, has declined from over 70 per cent of the world's population 50 years ago to less than 10 per cent today, literacy has flourished with 85 per cent of the world's population being literate today. Every day over 300,000 people gain access to electricity for the first time, and 285,000 acquire clean drinking water. So while Trump may drive us mad, and we rightly worry about climate change and the threat of nuclear war with North Korea, we can also remember that over 100 million children's lives have been saved since 1990 because of vaccinations, improved nutrition and public health programs.[4]

As I reflect more deeply on the question of what gives me hope personally, I find that wanting to experience more of life and to do new things: writing projects, seeing my grandchildren, trips, my garden, inner work – all these give me hope and meaning. The critical dimension, I think, is an orientation toward the future; life is not yet done, there is more to do, more to learn, more to experience.

Victor Frankl, the founder of Logo Therapy and an inmate in a Nazi concentration camp for three years during the Second World War, came to this conclusion when he asked himself the question as to why some inmates survived the horrors of the camps, and others did not.[5] He found that survivors had a sense of purpose, of meaning in life. They had a deep desire to again meet a friend, or see a child, or they had a project they wanted to complete.

Out of this experience, Frankl maintained that human beings are motivated by a 'will to meaning', and that life has meaning under all circumstances, even under great suffering.[6] He suggested that human beings discover meaning in life through creating a work, writing an essay, building a school, starting a garden; through a deep meeting or encounter with other human beings, and through developing a learning attitude toward our own struggles and suffering.[7]

In his essays and in his famous book, *Man's Search for Meaning*, Frankl also states other principles which I think are fundamental to understanding the dynamics of hope. One of these is that each human being is unique and has something singular to offer the world, a mission and purpose which gives meaning to their existence. I call this sense of purpose and direction my life path, my biography, my destiny; and it is usually made manifest to me through requests, meetings and conversations with others. That is also why Frankl suggests that one should not search for an abstract meaning in life, but should respond concretely and specifically to those demands, requests and opportunities which life presents.

Another profound insight came from Frankl's experience of hopelessness on a dark night while communing with his absent wife, and pondering what was the purpose of his suffering and slow death in the concentration camp.

> The guard passed by, insulting me, and once again I communed with my beloved. More and more I felt that she was present, that she was with

me; I had the feeling that I was able to touch her, able to stretch out my hand and grasp hers. Then at that very moment a bird flew down silently and perched just in front of me, on the heap of soil which I had dug up out of the ditch, and looked steadily at me.

This and similar experiences helped him to recognize that 'the salvation of man is through love and in love'.[8]

Listening to a medical doctor giving a talk about health many years ago confirmed my deep appreciation for Frankl's work. The doctor, Tom Cowan, said that he asked his patients three questions: are you on an inner path of moral and spiritual development; do you love someone; and do you like your work? He felt that if they answered all three in the affirmative, they were likely to be healthy. Is this because by affirming life and giving it meaning in these three ways, they had hope and were therefore more likely to be healthy? Certainly, having a metaphysical, religious or spiritual framework gives meaning, as does loving others and exercising compassion; and if we like our work then we are engaged in manifesting something in the world which gives us pleasure and an individual sense of purpose.

In summarizing these reflections on the nature of hope, I would say that built into human nature is the will to meaning, that we are beings of body, soul and spirit, and experience the world through these dimensions of our being, and that each of us can over time develop a deep sense of our uniqueness, of our life path. I see these dimensions of life as the foundation for hope as a force of the human soul, and as an essential orientation of the heart and spirit.

What Undermines Hope?

I recently watched Ai We We's documentary film 'Human Flow', and was again shocked and moved by the plight of refugees around the world: the Palestinians who have lived in camps in Lebanon for generations, or those from Syria stuck in Turkish settlements without the protection of international legal agreements, or those living in abandoned airline hangars in Berlin, without homes, community or work. Over 60 million people are now harbored in camps globally, fleeing war, terrorism, genocide or starvation. It seems to me that hope is difficult to sustain in these situations, and in those conditions which caused the flight of millions of people from their homeland in the first place.

If we recall Abraham Maslow's hierarchy of human needs, then the most basic needs are food, water, shelter and sanitation, or what are called 'physiological needs'.[9] A second category he identified as safety needs; freedom from discrimination, from racism, sexual harassment and violence, both physical and psychological. Reading Ta-Nehisi Coates' book *Between the World and Me* left me reflecting on what it must be like to fear being attacked, either from gangs or from the police, every morning when you leave home.[10] The many messages carried on the #Me Too hash-tag have helped me to recognize a similar fear associated with the sexual aggression and unwanted attention of men toward women, never mind the unending tales of discrimination against the LGBT community. In each of these situations, fear about our physical and psychological safety is at stake, pushing our consciousness to focus on safety and survival, and undermining our hope in the future.

The socially destructive impact of extreme inequalities of wealth around the globe is another factor which undermines hope by limiting health, fostering addictions, increasing crime, promoting violence and undermining democracy, as the research of Richard Wilkinson and Kate Pickett showed some years ago.[11] These effects were described in detail in my earlier essay 'Toxic Excess: Income Inequalities and the Fundamental Social Law' (Chapter 7, this volume).[12] If 40 per cent of the American public have no savings for retirement, and 60 per cent would have difficulty meeting an unexpected bill of $600, many more people in the USA than we normally assume are living close to the edge, and having to worry about feeding their children and paying their rent. Living in such a situation over time, with its accompanying feelings of shame, is a major contributor to the opioid epidemic affecting the small towns and cities across America. The situation is often exponentially worse in parts of Africa, Asia and Latin America, where inequalities of income and pervasive natural disasters combine to breed despair.

A very different dimension of modern life which undermines hope is made visible by the Korean-born German philosopher, Byung Chul Han. He describes Western society as a *Burnout Society*, in which isolation from others, alienation from the world and powerlessness to make changes in life result from the excessive stimuli of the electronic age, the performance focus of work, and the scattered consciousness of multi-tasking. Stress, depression, hyperactivity, narcissism, tiredness and addiction result from the achievement society creating a narcissistic subject incapable of meeting others and the world: 'Achievement society is the society of self-exploitation. The achievement subject exploits itself until it is burnt out.

In the process it develops auto-aggression that often enough escalates into the violence of self-destruction.'[13]

Han describes the modern human being as cut off from others and from community, with the result that the higher psychological and spiritual needs described by Maslow cannot be experienced, never mind met, as consciousness is focused on satisfying the cravings of addiction. These more philosophical insights are strongly supported by the work of Robert Lustig, the life styles and food researcher, who cites compelling evidence to prove the addictive nature of food (sugar), of drugs and medicine, and of the electronic media, as each gives us a dopamine hit which captures our body and our mind so that we are truly 'hacked' while filling the coffers of big Pharma and the computer and entertainment industries.[14]

Then there are the frequent delusions of false fears and hopes: Mexicans are murderers and rapists, Muslims are terrorists, immigrants are dangerous... – and so arises the false hope of build a wall, or stop immigration from Muslim countries, and make it generally hard for foreigners to come here at all. Meanwhile, white domestic terrorism is not so easily acknowledged. How many people still recall Aurora, Colorado or Timothy McVeigh, and the Oklahoma City bombing which killed 168 people and wounded over 600 in April of 1995?

Lastly, I want to mention the undermining of truth, of scientific research and the creation of 'fake news', as an effort by some political and economic elites to undermine the possibility of democratic discourse, of a genuine conversation between well-meaning people concerned about the future. It is profoundly demoralizing, and undermines hope when there is no longer a common basis of factual and moral truth, when relativity and personal opinion replace reasoned argument, poisoning the well of civic dialogue and tearing apart families and communities.

Practicing Hope

Hope is also a practice, or rather a set of practices. As Joanna Macy argues,'Like tai chi or gardening it is something we do rather than have'.[15] It is both an orientation of the heart and a practice of the will, which gives meaning and purpose to our lives. What I have found particularly helpful in fostering active hope in my life are the following kinds of actions. As you follow along in your mind, please also note those activities, those practices, which have sustained your hope and which you can recommend to others.

Creating Moments of Inner Quiet and Reflection

Robert Coles once remarked, 'We should look inward and think about the meaning of our life and its purposes, lest we do it in twenty or thirty years and it's too late'.[16] If we can find a few minutes every day to sit quietly and ponder our life, its questions and its joys and sorrows, we can come to ourselves, honoring the need which Byung Chul Han identifies as a tragic lack in our addicted society, the need for quiet contemplation. In taking this time we find ourselves as an 'I' capable of seeing and bearing the injustices and pain of the world and an 'I' capable of helping.

Doing Biography Work

If we remember Frankl's insight that life has meaning, and that each individual has a unique purpose and mission, then reflecting systematically upon the patterns, themes and meanings built into our life journey, into our biography, can be of enormous assistance in finding our bearings and in unleashing our creativity. My first memory as a young child was of a daylight air-raid in Germany during the Second World War. Much later I experienced the military confrontation in Berlin in 1961 between Russian, American and British troops during the building of the wall. The theme of war and peace, of conflict and healing, have been part of my life journey, leading me to study international politics and engaging in conflict resolution and social transformation work. I believe each of our lives contains such patterns and themes which have meanings that can be unlocked through reflection, and through art. This is what a biography workshop or a biography working group can offer to its participants, and in the process it also awakens a deep interest in the life journey of others.[17]

Seeing the Good

I am struck by the generosity of people and their effort to do the good, as I have repeatedly pointed out in these essays. During times of crisis, the recent earthquake in Mexico City, Katrina in New Orleans, or during 9/11– people came together, supported each other and honored community. We can carry this awareness of the basic goodness of people as a talisman against the cynicism of the media, and also against the acts of cruelty which people do still carry out against nature and each other.

Recognizing the Gift in Daily Life

I also attempt to see the gift, the joyful experience, given to me every day, if I can bring attention to it. It can be seeing a cardinal feeding its young, the warmth with which an elderly man wishes the pharmacist a Happy

Thanksgiving, or the giggles of two young children playing in the park. Our days contain many such gifts, and being aware and grateful for such offerings is a balm to the soul in these times. In the moment, recognize the gift and meet it with gratitude, or recall it in the evening as you think about the day, and give thanks.

Appreciating Nature
Appreciating the patterns and beauty of nature is also a daily practice for me. The geese flying north in spring stirs joy and confidence. The joyful arrival of the robins in late March and the crimson of the sugar maples in October remind me of earth's gifts, as does the geometric unfolding of the ferns and the crystal lattice of the frost on my bedroom window in February.

Practicing Moral Discernment
As I have previously suggested, I believe we live in a moral universe, and that many of the issues we confront, and read about, are present in our life and consciousness in order to wake us up morally and spiritually. By this I do not mean that we can automatically apply a moral commandment from the Bible, the Koran or the Talmud, but rather that we need to carry moral responsibility for how we lead our life, use our resources, and think and act in the world. The time for relying on outside authority, or established moral maxims, is receding, and we are each faced with the challenge of what is the good in this situation, and how do I support it? This extends to what food, cars and products I buy, what causes I support humanly and financially, what news I watch and the media to which I give attention, and what books I read, what I think about and how I live my life from day to day.

As mentioned in an earlier essay, for me 'the good' includes that which fosters freedom and community among people, diversity of viewpoints and cultural forms, the quality of caring in relationships and work, and being a responsible steward of the earth. Its opposite is that which enhances egotism, exploitation of people and the earth, manipulation of information, the blind pursuit of power and everything which undermines the dignity of human beings and all life forms. An economic system which exploits people, communities and the earth's resources for profit and control is immoral, and a political system which promotes 'one dollar, one vote' is corrupt.

I agree with Christopher Frye, the English poet and playwright who, in *The Sleep of Prisoners*, has Burgeon say, 'Thank God our time is now when wrong comes up to face us everywhere…. Affairs are now soul size….'.[18] Our thoughts, feelings and actions matter, as individuals and groups, because they affect the moral and ethical order of the universe. We cannot complain about environmental pollution and throw plastic bottles out the window, or lament the growing gap between rich and poor if we are not willing to pay people working for us a living wage. We are called upon to bear witness to the times we live in, and also to lead our lives as if the society we long for is already present now. The more we practice this – the implementing and enacting of our values in life, and also acknowledging our failures to do so – the more I think hope is alive in our soul and in the world.

The Journey of Hope and Transformation

A few years ago Robert Macfarlane wrote a wonderful book about journeying over the paths and lanes of England and Scotland, as well as other localities, communing with nature and himself. He remarks on the increase in pilgrims and pilgrimages, 'the hinterlands were filling with eccentrics, making their odd journeys in the belief that certain voyages out might become voyages in'.[19] Many of us, millions in fact, have become eccentric pilgrims on an outer and inner journey to bring healing to the world, and to ourselves. We have become part of the 'Blessed Unrest', many Don Quixotes, who do not accept the corruption of our institutions, the threats to the earth, and the suffering of our brothers and sisters without attempting reform. And this means going on a journey of outer and inner transformation.

All journeys proceed in stages, and pilgrimages contain both an inner and an outer quest. If I reflect on my experiences in seeking to help organizations and groups as well as in starting initiatives, I find the journey begins with attention to what the world is asking of me or inviting me to be engaged in, and gratitude for what has been given to me in the past as capacities, work and life. Both seem equally important: without attention to the question and issue, there is no journey to go on; and without gratitude toward life we lack the nourishment and inner strength to undertake the pilgrimage. What led David Isay to start the non-profit called Storycorps in 2003, to set up a listening booth in Grand Central Station where people could share their life stories and questions with each other, and then to publish some of the resulting stories in a best-selling book, *Listening Is an Act of Love* in 2007? What moved the WNBA star Tina

Charles to establish Hopey's Heart Foundation and to donate much of her salary to the purchase of external defibrillators for the athletic programs of many schools?[20] Something moved them to take a step, to try something in response to a need – attention – and to have the courage to take a step into the unknown – confidence based on gratitude for life and its opportunities.

In their stimulating book on social change, Otto Scharmer and Katrin Kaufer describe the beginning of the presencing process by stating that 'energy follows attention', while Joanna Macy and Chris Johnstone talk about gratitude as the essential starting point of a journey they call the work that reconnects.[21] In their book *Active Hope*, they outline a journey in four stages: 'Coming from Gratitude, Honoring our Pain for the World, Seeing with New Eyes, and Going Forth'. I recognize five sequential phases when reflecting on social change projects and activities with which I have been involved. The first of these I have called 'attention to the world and its needs' – needs which knock on the door of our soul, and as an inner soul mood, positivity and gratitude for being given the chance to make a difference, for being able to work on this question. While it may seem somewhat perverse to imagine feeling gratitude for being able to work on an issue which burdens humanity, we can remember Frankl's insight, hope stems from life having meaning, and giving to others out of compassion and with humility gives us such meaning.

I then experience four further stages, partially described in an earlier essay titled 'Witnessing the Long Emergency' (Chapter 1, this volume). The second step is that of gaining insight and understanding of the questions and issues at stake. In the presencing process described by Scharmer and Kaufer, this is described as seeking to have an open mind, with the injunction: *observe, observe, observe*. One could add 'learn, learn, learn' as much as possible, while keeping an open mind about relationships, causes and possible solutions.

When working with organizations I also attempt to build as complete a picture of the situation as possible, interviewing people and exploring the history and biography of the institution. By keeping an open mind and not quickly judging a situation, and paying attention to little things, totally new dimensions appear. In one situation the school's sign was small, badly made and partially obscured by a bush, leading me to explore with teachers and Board whether they really valued Waldorf education and had confidence in their school. In a home for people with special needs, everyone appeared exhausted, and buildings and grounds were not well maintained – leading to the discovery that daily and weekly rhythms were irregular, and scheduling was truly chaotic.

The third step I think of as that of developing empathy, letting the struggles, failings and sufferings of society and of our brothers and sisters into my soul. We tend to want to keep things at arm's length, objective and rational; and yet letting into our heart the drought and starvation in Africa, the plight of refugees in Lebanon, the stuck leadership group in a company, or the struggle of immigrants in our community, is a very important step in our being able to help. To hold, to let in, and not to condemn, judge or belittle.

For Scharmer and Katrin Kaufer this is the step of the 'Open Heart', and for Joanna Macy and Chris Johnstone it is 'honoring the pain of the world', as well as our own pain. The German word 'Mitleid' expresses the essential nature of this third step because it literally means 'living the pain of the other'.

Christine Gruwez calls this step one of inwardness, of a deep listening by creating an open and listening heart. She says, 'In other words we let the events that are acted out on the world stage deeply within us, so deeply that it might be said that we make them part of our own being'.[22] I practice this step by creating inner pictures and letting them come alive in myself. In an earlier essay I described working inwardly with Syrian refuges stuck at the Hungarian border in winter, a young ISIL fighter in Mosul awaiting his certain death, and the African American youth alone and struggling with aids in rural Mississippi. More recently I have added the fires on the US west coast, imagining what it must be like to be poised for flight and have your bags packed at all times. I also attempt a similar picturing process in myself with client groups when doing advisory work, trying to deepen my empathy for the issues and struggles they are experiencing and withholding criticism and blame. This effort to open my heart, if done earnestly, then awakens and deepens my will to help, and lends intuitive guidance to my work.

The fourth step is that of willing, of doing the work of transformation, which Scharmer and Kaufer call 'open will', and Joanna Macy and Chris Johnstone describe as 'going forth'. You can join the work of environmental preservation (Trustees of Reservation or 360.org), women's rights (Code Pink), legal rights (ACLU, NAACP), mediation and conflict resolution (Doctors without Borders, Karuna Center for Peacebuilding) and a host of other causes; local, national and international. We give our time and our money to make a better world. We also, with others, develop alternatives to existing institutions and practices.

Discouraged and upset by the role of the banking industry in the financial crisis of 2008 (see 'The Crisis of Western Capitalism' (Chapter 4) and 'Common-Sense Outrage' (Chapter 6), this volume), a group of friends and I created the Berkshire Columbia Investment Network (BCIN) to provide short- and medium-term loans to local businesses and organizations who could not get conventional bank financing. Dr Mike Rosmann, an Iowa farmer and trained psychologist, was stunned by the suicide rate of farmers during the agricultural crisis of the late 1980s – nearly twice the rate of returning veterans – because of their isolation, independence and the cost of medical care and insurance in rural areas. So he started a hotline movement in the agricultural states of the Mid West, and now heads Sowing Seeds of Hope, a non-profit group that trains medical professionals for working with farmers, runs hotline services in seven states, and has provided medical and counseling services to over 100,000 farm families in the last decade.[23]

You have done likewise by supporting or starting groups and initiatives seeking a better world, and by so doing you too have been on this journey of hope and transformation, on this outer and inner pilgrimage.

The fifth step I would describe as joining and building community, for when we support a cause or start an initiative, we are joining with others to do the good. The resulting sense of human connection fosters mutual creativity, strengthens hope, and gives us the stamina to persist, to exercise the long will. It also asks us to practice the values we espouse in our relationship with others, calling us to the task of building beloved community.

I have summarized these steps on the Journey of Hope and Transformation in the diagram below:

Attention to the Issues — GRATITUDE
Gaining Insight — ABIDING INTEREST
Developing Empathy — DEEP CARING
Focused Willing — LOVING ACTION
Building Community — CO-CREATION

Figure 1 Steps on the Journey of Hope and Transformation

This journey is both an outer and an inner pilgrimage. The outer pilgrimage begins with an issue: women's rights, income inequalities, or the resettlement of refugees, or how to help a group or organization and then through understanding, empathy and acting in concert with others, we attempt to bring healing and resolution. The inner journey is to transform the cynicism, doubt, judgement and egotism in our soul, by developing interest (open mind), deep caring (open heart) and loving action (open will). Seeking to bring healing and transformation to the world is at the same time a road to our own salvation, helping us to overcome the materialistic, egotistical and fear-based consciousness of the Western mindset.

Like all true pilgrimages, this journey builds a more loving heart.

Notes

1   Vaclav Havel, 'The kind of hope I often think about', in *Disturbing the Peace*, Vintage Books, New York, 1990, p. 181.
2   Martin Luther King, Sermon at Wesleyan University, 1964, also mentioned during various civil rights marches in 1966, including in Selma, Alabama.
3   Yoval Noah Hazan, *Homo Deus*, Vintage, New York, 2017, pp. 3–24.
4   Nicholas Kristof, 'Good news, despite what you have heard', *New York Times*, 2 July 2017.
5   Victor Frankl, *Man's Search for Meaning: An Introduction to Logotherapy*, Simon and Schuster, New York, 1972, pp. 153–154.
6   Frankl, p. 165.
7   Frankl, p. 176.
8   Frankl, p. 64.
9   Abraham Maslow, 'A theory of human motivation', in *Psychological Review*, 1943. There has been a long and interesting conversation about the nature of motivation among psychologists. Maslow's Hierarchy of Needs, with the now famous pyramid of lower and higher needs, has been foundational for this debate. See also Daniel Pink, *Drive*, Riverhead Books, Penguin, New York, 2009, which supports Frankl in suggesting that what motivates us are the same things which give us hope.
10   Ta-Nehisi Coates, *Between the World and Me*, Spiegel and Gauer, New York, 2015.
11   Richard Wilkinson and Kate Pickett, *The Spirit Level: Why Greater Equality Makes Societies Stronger*, Bloomsbury Press, London, New York, 2010, pp. 49–173. Groundbreaking research!
12   See the essay, 'Toxic Excess: Income Inequalities and the Fundamental Social Law', Chapter 7 in this book.
13   Byung Chul Han, *Burn Out Society*, Stanford University Press, Palo Alto, Calif., 2015, p. 47. Stimulating and perplexing in the tradition of European hermeneutics.
14   Robert Lustig, *The Hacking of the American Mind*, Penguin/Random House, New York, 2017, pp. 1–45.
15   Joanna Macy and Chris Johnstone, *Active Hope: How to Face the Mess We're in without Going Crazy*, New World Library, Novato, Calif., 2012, p. 3.
16   Robert Coles, interview with *People Magazine*, 24 December 1990.
17   See www.biographysocialart.org.
18   Christopher Fry, *A Sleep of Prisoners*, Oxford University Press, New York, 1951.
19   Robert Macfarlane, *The Old Ways: A Journey on Foot*, Penguin Books, London, 2013, pp. 235–236.
20   Otto Scharmer and Katrin Kaufer, *Leading from the Emerging Future: From Ego System to Eco System Economies*, Berrett-Koehler, Oakland, Calif., 2013, p. 21. See also Macy and Johnstone, *Active Hope*, p. 6.
21   See 'Toxic Excess', Chapter 7 in this volume.
22   An inspiring meditation on the nature of our times – Christine Gruwez, *Walking with Your Time: A Manichean Journey*, Lulu, 2011, p. 74.
23   Debbie Weingarten, 'Why are American farmers killing themselves in record numbers?', The *Guardian*, 6 December 2017.

Chapter 10

The Pattern and Ideology of Oppression
(June 2018)

Unlimited power is apt to corrupt the minds of those who possess it.

William Pitt, the Elder

I The Pattern of Oppression: The Corruption and Decline of a Once-Great Nation

Throughout these essays I have argued that as American citizens we have allowed political, cultural and economic elites to manipulate us in order to pursue their own wealth and visions of power at our expense, leading to the corruption and decline of a once-great nation. Sadly, we only seem to have a limited awareness of this decline and of its causes, and are now living in growing fear of an unstable president and an irresponsible and corrupt Congress.

In summarizing my reflections on how our nation has been undermined and weakened, I am painting a bleak picture, suggesting that there is a direct link between our aggressive foreign policy, 9/11, the War on Terror, the economic crisis and the Presidency of Donald Trump. They are each, and in sequence, manifestations of the American shadow or 'double', in which power and wealth have undermined the better nature of our people and our culture. It is as Martin Luther King said over 50 years ago, 'We as a nation must undergo a radical revolution of values.... A nation that continues year after year to spend more money on military defense than on programs of social justice is approaching spiritual death.'[1] If the resistance to Donald Trump and everything he embodies recognizes that the problems we face are much deeper than the personality and policies of a president, that they represent a spiritual, social, political and economic malaise, calling for a re-imagining of America for our time, then there is hope for our future. The beginning of such a journey of healing and transformation is to recognize clearly what has happened, and how we have been lied to and misled into believing an ideology of oppression.

In reading through a narrative which focuses on our failings and is a short summary of previous chapters, I ask you to remember that there is no shadow without light, that the American dream still lives in large numbers of people both here and abroad. It is as the philosopher and historian Jacob Needleman noted in his study of *The American Soul* – 'America was once the hope of the world...', and it is still 'the fact, the symbol and the promise of a new beginning', if we find the courage and the heart to make it so.[2]

The American Empire Project

I have presented arguments and evidence to suggest that following the collapse of the Soviet system in Russia and Eastern Europe in 1989, the first Bush administration ignored the opportunities afforded by the demise of the Soviet Union and of the bi-polar world, and instead developed a strategic plan for expanding American global power with Dick Cheney as Secretary of Defense, and Colin Powell as Head of the Joints Chief of Staff. These plans were primarily articulated by Paul Wolfowitz, and found expression in the Defense Planning Documents for 1994–1999 and the Defense Strategy for the 1990s. They were supported by the neo-conservative wings of both the Republican and Democratic parties, the Christian Right, Conservative think-tanks such as the American Enterprise Institute and even the Council on Foreign Relations. The rationale and principles behind these plans were first articulated by Samuel Huntington in *The Clash of Civilizations and the Remaking of World Order*, and by Henry Kissinger and Zbigniew Brzezinski, the three senior statesmen of the American foreign policy establishment. These principles were then tested during the first US invasion of Iraq, Desert Storm, in 1991.[3]

With the eight years of the Clinton administration, 1992–2000, the aggressive tendencies of the American Empire Project were muted by the more multilateral orientation of the new president and his staff, and the complexity of the Balkan Crisis. However, the neo-conservatives continued their planning through the Project for a New American Century (PNAC), founded by Irving Crystal and Robert Kagan and joined by Cheney, Wolfowitz, Powell, Rumsfeld and a large number of other political and economic luminaries from both the Republican and Democratic parties. With the election of George W. Bush in 2000, Cheney became vice president, Powell, Secretary of State, and Rumsfeld Secretary of Defense. The neo-conservatives were thus again in full control of both US foreign policy and the Department of Defense, while Cheney guided a hapless George W. Bush and his new administration.

The administration and its neo-conservative supporters recognized that they needed something like a 'New Pearl Harbor' to mobilize the American electorate in favor of more foreign military adventures in pursuit of extending American power, as suggested by the Project for a New American Century. And strangely, just that happened on 9/11.

The event of 9/11 provided the justification for the attack on Afghanistan and the later invasion and occupation of Iraq, as well as for the creation of the National Security State and the increases in our already-large defense budget. George W. Bush stated on 12 September 2001, 'The deliberate and deadly attacks which were carried out yesterday against our country were more than acts of terror... – this will be a monu-mental struggle of good versus evil.'[4] And so the 'War on Terror' began.

Like 30 per cent of Americans and many international observers of American politics, I believe that some members of the US government colluded or hid essential information in support of the attacks on the World Trade Center and the Pentagon. I have cited evidence to support this view, and suggested that an independent investigation is vital for any healing of the American soul, as the many official lies about 9/11 have contributed to the malaise, and the deep divisions amongst the American public.[5]

The War on Terror, unleashed after 9/11 and pursued over the last 16 years by Bush, Obama and now Trump, has been a great disaster for America and the world, leading to:

- the chaos and violence in the Middle East with the killing and displace-ment of millions of people in Afghanistan, Libya, Syria, Iraq, Yemen, Egypt and parts of northern and central Africa;
- the creation of a militant Islam in its many forms, and a widening conflict between Sunni and Shia groups and nations;
- a flood of refugees seeking to find new homes in Europe and other parts of the world, destabilizing the European Union and leading to the UK's Brexit vote, as well as to the rise of a racist, fascist, white nationalism;
- endless unsuccessful wars with no clear outcomes, at the astronomical expense of $5 trillion – money which could have been spent on

education, renewing infrastructure, universal health-care and aiding
the declining industries of the American manufacturing sector;

- the undermining of American democracy and the constitution with
the extension of executive privilege, a culture of secrecy, the illegal
spying on both US citizens and foreign leaders, and the militarization
of American police forces through the gifting of excess military hard-
ware to cities and towns;

- a global culture of fear and manipulation in which refugees, Muslims,
Mexicans, people of color and foreigners become the other, justifying
the use of violence and the limitation of human rights;

- the killing and wounding of the young in the Middle East and elsewhere, including wounded GIs and those returning home suffering
from Post-traumatic Stress Disorder; and

- the financial collapse of 2008–10.[6]

The Global Economic Crisis

The United States initiated the War on Terror following the tragic events
of 9/11. It also carries primary responsibility for the global economic
crisis of 2008–10. As stated in a previous essay on 'The Crisis of Western
Capitalism' (Chapter 4):

> The immediate cause of the crisis is understood to be the failure of the
> sub-prime mortgage market and the related drop in home prices, but the
> true causes go much deeper: the deregulation of the financial markets
> beginning with Ronald Reagan, the easy money and low interest
> rate policies of the Federal Reserve under Alan Greenspan and his
> successors, the reckless and corrupt behavior of financial institutions
> and Wall Street firms, and most importantly, the increase in private,
> corporate and governmental debt during the last eight years of the Bush
> administration. Total outstanding US debt, private and public, had
> grown from $2 trillion in 1974 to over $44 trillion in 2006, and has
> increased markedly since then.[7]

The 'War on Terror', the increased levels of defense spending and the
wars in Afghanistan and Iraq played a significant role in unleashing the
economic crisis through the further expansion of governmental debt.

After the presidential election of 2008, the new Obama administration
and the Democrats were left holding the bag of the economic recession, and
had to further increase government debt in order to bail out the financial
industry which was largely responsible for the crisis in the first place,

along with the automobile industry. The average American, in particular inner-city residents and working-class communities, paid the price of corruption in Washington and New York, with effective unemployment reaching 16 per cent in 2009, while median family net worth dropped by more than half, from $119,000 in 2007 to just $66,000 in 2013.[8]

Income and Wealth Inequalities in the United States

Recently, hedge-fund manager Ray Dalio stated that income inequalities are 'the biggest issue of our time, the biggest economic issue, the biggest political issue and the biggest social issue'.[9] As the United States has the highest income and wealth inequalities of any Western society, on a par with Turkey, Argentina and Thailand, income inequalities are certainly a searing indictment of our economic and political system. The reason for this is that high levels of inequality are associated with poorer health outcomes and higher health care costs, more addiction and increased levels of mental instability, higher crime rates and higher prison populations, as well as more police and security personnel, as was described in my 'Toxic Excess' essay (Chapter 7).

We have become a nation of 'somebodies and nobodies', to use Robert Fuller's apt phrase, with the top 1 per cent of the country controlling over 40 per cent of the nation's wealth, and the bottom 80 per cent just 7 per cent. Such inequalities have not been seen in the United States since just before the Great Depression, suggesting that we again live in a plutocracy where wealthy elites skew the political and economic decision-making process to favor the rich – or as Joseph Stiglitz, the Nobel Prize winning economist, noted, our tax and other policies reflect 'of the 1%, by the 1% and for the 1%' (see Chapter 7, note 16). The recent tax overhaul by the Republican-controlled House and Senate in December 2017 will only increase these inequalities, and further extend corporate control over the public agenda and of government. It will also further increase private and public debt, erode the middle class and increase authoritarian appeals to solving our nation's problems.

Undermining Democracy

In the last decades our society has drifted a long way from the ideals of a democratic society, as there have been multiple actions to weaken our democracy and undermine the principle of 'one person, one vote'. Giving corporations the power to give unlimited amounts of money to political parties, candidates and political action committees, as was cynically done by the Supreme Court in the Citizens United (2010), is the most egregious example, adding overt political inequality to the inequality of wealth, income and opportunity. With declining union membership and the astronomical cost of political campaigns, corporations and wealthy individuals are the main sources of political funding – with the inevitable result that the political, economic, tax and social priorities of the wealthy are honored, and that of the working class, of the poor and of minority groups and individuals, ignored. Gerrymandering election districts, increasing eligibility requirements, purging voter rolls of minorities, holding elections during working hours, and having ill-functioning voting machines and inadequate voting facilities are additional ways in which political parties, primarily the GOP, undermine the political rights of citizens.

We should also not forget the cynical movement of politicians from Congress to the lobbying firms of K Street, nor the manipulation, lying and fear-mongering of the media in the age of terror and surveillance. Can we still say we live in a democracy in the United States, in Britain or in many other countries, when 'one dollar (pound), one vote' has increasingly replaced 'one person, one vote'?

The Environmental Crisis in the Anthropocene Age

The Trump administration's withdrawal from the Paris Climate Accords, its roll-back of environmental regulation and its opening of the Arctic and US coastal waters to oil drilling, shows the utter contempt which the corporate-controlled Congress and administration have for the American public and, more importantly, for the future of the earth. These actions are such outrageous examples of the naked, short-term self-interest embedded in the ideas of the Neo-Liberal Economic Agenda underlying our economic system that it takes my breath away. As astrobiologist Allan Grinspoon mentions, 'I think our fundamental Anthropocene dilemma is that we have achieved global impact but have no means for global self-control'.[10] All markers of global warming, species extinction of both plants and animals, polar loss of ice, and sea-level rise, are exceeding the predictions made even a few years ago, leading many environmentalists to despair about our future.

A Painful Reflection

It seems to me that the environmental crisis, and an American government which threatens world peace and undermines the well-being of its own people, call for deep and painful reflection. I think the widespread belief in American exceptionalism – that we are a Beacon on the Hill, a

New Jerusalem, the defender of democracy and freedom – has become the vain illusion of a people and a society unable to see its own darker nature; its shadow of racism, economic exploitation, nationalism and militarism, built into its history and so frightfully evident in the connected crises just described. I share the mood of Republican Congressman Walter Jones Jr. who asks, 'are we in the final days of a great nation?' in which our immorality, aggression, blindness and lack of gratitude bring on the destruction described in the Book of Revelations.[11]

I deeply fear that some form of governmental complicity in 9/11 occurred. If so, it would represent such a deep betrayal of the core values of America that I would see it as a kind of spiritual suicide, undermining our healthier, more open, caring and human nature as a society and a people, and unleashing the forces of greed, prejudice, aggression and war which we are now witnessing with such force. If such a betrayal occurred, it has freed the forces of our double, of our shadow side as a nation, to plague the world and ourselves. If four US presidents and administrations can consistently lie about Vietnam, knowing it was an unwinnable war, and sacrifice over two million Vietnamese and over 60,000 GIs to save face, could the Bush/Cheney administration not have lied about 9/11, promoting a false narrative about what actually happened?

If this did indeed occur, then the title of David Ray Griffin's new book, *Bush and Cheney: How They Ruined America and the World*, is apt and the election of Donald Trump as president a fitting commentary on our times.[12] We have come home and occupied ourselves by electing a lying, narcissistic, ill-tempered, misogynistic, racist, uncultured but clever fool, thereby truly expressing aspects of what we have become. So how can we recover something of our better nature and create a society of greater peace, equality and abundance? How can we heal ourselves from the allure of seeking ever-greater power over others, other nations, other people and over an earth that is reeling from our self-centered and profit-driven assault?

II The Ideology of Oppression

I think the first step toward healing is to recognize the operating values on which our economic, political and international state systems are now largely based, for the social world *is* us, reflecting our values, ideas and priorities, no matter how unconscious we are about this creation process. Social and economic ideas and practices are not neutral in their effect on our behavior, our consciousness or our well-being. I previously noted Keynes's insight that it is ideas which ultimately matter for good or evil in the world. But the insight is ancient, and is well expressed in the Buddhist teaching:

> Watch your thoughts
> They become words,
> Watch your words,
> They become deeds,
> Watch your deeds,
> They become habits,
> Watch your habits,
> They become character.[13]

What we think and believe, we articulate, and then enact and indeed, over time, become. Put another way, we create society and it, in turn, creates us. Edgar Cayce, the American psychic, put this succinctly by stating, 'the mind is the maker'; and Rudolf Steiner, the Austrian educator and philosopher, added, 'we all resemble the God we understand'.[14]

The Rationale for War: The Principles of Realpolitik and the American Empire Project

In describing the genesis and evolution of the American Empire Project from 1990 to the present day, I mentioned the formative influence of neo-Conservative thought in American foreign policy, when married to the millennial beliefs of the Christian Right and the principles of Great Power Politics so clearly articulated by Henry Kissinger and others.[15] These principles of Realpolitik are one strand of the ideology of oppression. They include:

- A great nation must have a long-term global foreign policy which maximizes its power and influence in the world.
- In pursuing such a policy it must have sufficient economic and military power to defeat at least two of its great power rivals at any one time.
- A great power must promote regional conflicts and rivalries, always maintaining a key balancing role. (Balance of Power Politics.) Think China/Taiwan, India/Pakistan, Israel/Iran, Russia/Western Europe, Saudi Arabia/Iran.
- Democracies are not effective in the conduct of foreign affairs, being easily swayed by popular opinion, therefore information must be managed and true interests and strategies hidden from a fickle public.

- A great power must occasionally go to war, otherwise the threat of force is not credible in the conduct of foreign affairs. US involvement in military campaigns and in the clandestine overthrow of governments since the Second World War is legion; Korea, Iran, Greece, Vietnam, Panama, Guatemala, Nicaragua, Chile, Haiti, Yugoslavia, Lebanon, Libya, Afghanistan and Iraq are the better-known examples.
- War is essential for the survival of the State, to protect itself from other aggressive states and ideologies, and in order to control the unruly elements of one's own population.

Since the 1980s these principles have been linked with the millennial prophecies of the Christian Right, and the neo-conservative commitment to projecting power in the Middle East and around the world, a commitment given extra energy by the perceived imperatives of the War on Terror. We have been at war more or less continually since 1941, and in Afghanistan since 2001, and in Iraq since 2003, at a total cost of between $4 and 7.1 trillion for these latter wars, depending on how costs and interest are calculated.[16] Our annual defense budget, which does not include all costs associated with the wars in the Middle East and Afghanistan, was $571 billion in 2017, and is projected to be $700 billion in 2018, much more than the defense budgets of China and Russia combined. The largely unrecognized ideology of great power politics has driven the United States to pursue a global empire strategy from the time of the Cold War to the present day, at the cost of millions of lives and, I believe, at the cost of the social health of our society.

Neoliberal Ideology
A second strand of the intellectual and value-based ideology of oppression is neoliberalism. As George Monbiot commented in the *Guardian*:

> Its anonymity is both a symptom and a cause of its power. It has played a major role in a variety of crises: the financial meltdown of 2007–8, the offshoring of wealth and power, of which the Panama Papers offer us merely a glimpse, the slow collapse of public health and education, resurgent child poverty, the epidemic of loneliness, the collapse of ecosystems and the rise of Donald Trump.[17]

Dominant since the Reagan/Thatcher years, neoliberalism is an ideology which justifies shrinking government, reducing taxes, privatizing services, deregulating markets and globalizing the economy. It also advocates a heartless approach to the old, the poor and the less fortunate, for if you are not doing well it is your fault for lacking the skill, the character or the good fortune for thriving in a meritocracy.

As I wrote after the financial crisis in 2009, the principles of this ideology were clearly identified by David Korten when he described the reigning belief system of neoliberalism in *When Corporations Rule the World*:

- 'sustained economic growth as measured by the gross domestic product is the path to human progress'.
- Competition and 'free markets, unrestrained by government, generally result in the most efficient allocation of resources'.
- 'Economic globalization, achieved by removing barriers to the free flow of goods and money anywhere in the world, spurs competition, increases consumer choice, increases economic growth and is generally beneficial to everyone.
- Privatization, which moves functions and assets from government to the private sector, improves efficiency.
- The primary responsibility of government is to provide the infrastructure necessary to advance commerce and to enforce the rule of law with respect to property rights and contracts.'[18]

There is a variety of objections one can make to this ideology of competition and exploitation. It denigrates the public sector, does not acknowledge the real limitations of markets, and extols the virtues of competition rather than those of co-operation. Perhaps most importantly, it sees the production and consumption of goods and services as the most important function of society and, indeed, of human life.

Undermining Democracy

The third aspect of the ideology of oppression is the previously mentioned perversion and undermining of democratic ideals. The ideal of 'one person, one vote', irrespective of race, class, religion or philosophical/ political persuasion, is widely regarded as the birthright of citizens in Western democracies. Yet from the founding of the United States we have had a deep fear of the masses, initially limiting the vote to white propertied men, and then only with great struggle extending it to other races and to women. It is easy to forget that the Senate, until about a hundred years ago, was appointed by the state legislatures, representing propertied interests. Since the late 1960s, and partly in response to the opposition to the Vietnam War and the challenges posed to the system by both the civil-rights movement and the emerging counter-culture, a multi-faceted attack on democratic values has occurred. This is not openly admitted, since to do so would be to undermine the illusion that we live in a free, equal and democratic society. However, I believe that the operating as opposed to the espoused values of many political and economic elites about the political process include the following elements:

- **The aim of politics is to exercise power through controlling elections, legislation, government actions and the courts.** The famous Powell memorandum of 1971 to the US Chamber of Commerce warned American corporations that if they were not active politically and in education, they would lose their influence and freedom.[19] This warning was heeded and then made fully operational by Citizens United, a Supreme Court decision in 2010, allowing corporations to give unlimited amounts of money to politicians, political parties, research institutes and to special interest groups in the name of free speech. The power of the gun lobby, the NRA, to block sensible gun legislation in the United States, despite the horrendous record of gun violence and widespread support for more effective gun-control measures, is a testament to the efficacy of this view.

- **In the American 'democratic system', power can best be exercised through financial donations to political parties, political action committees and to candidates by corporations and the wealthy in order to determine both foreign and domestic policy, and in particular to control the nature of the legal and financial systems.** The support on corporate boards for large expenditures on political lobbying and financial donations to parties and candidates shows that such fees are seen as an essential cost of doing business in the United States; one that is fully justified by the results achieved. The anti-tax agenda of the Republican Party and the recently passed tax bill have lowered personal income taxes, corporate taxes and inheritance taxes to all-time lows at the expense of public well-being and genuine democracy.

- **The media in all of its forms allows well-funded interest groups to shape public opinion – to manufacture consent – and thereby to engineer elections according to their goals.** The public is only now beginning to wake up to the enormous power which media corporations such as Google, Microsoft, Facebook, Fox and other TV conglomerates have over our minds and lives, demonstrated by the Russian meddling in elections, and the collection of private information for marketing and surveillance purposes. The illegal use of private Facebook information for political purposes by Cambridge Analytica to support the election of Donald Trump in 2016 is a stark reminder of this threat. The power of advertising dollars to control the media and the national agenda cannot be underestimated, especially when it is connected to clever marketing. It is almost a hundred years since Edward Bernays, Sigmund Freud's nephew, was active developing the modern sales pitch, believing, as he did, that intelligent minorities need to make 'use of propaganda continuously and systematically' in order to control the imprudent masses'.[20]

• **A two-party system is ideally suited to channel the attitudes and emotions of the public toward left and right, polarizing the electorate, while diverting attention from the underlying injustices of society and hiding the true power of the wealthy and of corporations.** Any leftist critique of the system is socialist, foreign and coddles gays and immigrants, while truly conservative criticisms about government control of education, for example, are labeled as reactionary, racist and religious. Corporate control of the media means avoiding deeper discussions of meaningful economic and political reform.

• **A seemingly democratic society, as long as it allows the uncontrolled expenditure of money, a pay to play system, becomes a system of social control, avoiding the pitfalls of obviously totalitarian regimes.** A 2014 study by Martin Gilens and Benjamin Page showed that there is very little correlation between public attitudes and the policy decisions of state and national government in the United States, instead correlating closely with wealth and corporate interests. Their study demonstrates convincingly that the poorest 70 per cent of the population have next to no influence on government decisions, while the top 10 per cent have effective control.[21] Trump's victory was in part a reaction to this widespread and deeply felt recognition by the white working class and the Christian Evangelical Right.

• **Deny the distinctions of wealth and class and the reality of corporate power, and weaken any challenge to the power of corporations, whether by unions, political parties or co-operative enterprises, and veto legislation holding corporations accountable for environmental or human damages.** We have witnessed the successful socialization of risk for business, for example the bailout of the financial sector and the automobile industry by government during the financial crisis of 2007–9 and the privatization of public services and assets for the sake of corporate profit. The recent extensive leasing of federally and state-owned land to oil and energy companies and to the lumber industry for minimal cost is another dimension of the corporate control of politics.

- **Foster a sense of insecurity and fear amongst substantial parts of the population through an expensive inadequate medical insurance system, poor unemployment benefits, limited workers' rights and inadequate wages. Add to this, clearly identified foreign enemies – 'Islamic terrorists', Mexicans and the rivals to American hegemony, China, and Russia. Finally, point out domestic threats, whether Mexican immigrants, Muslims, Black Lives Matter advocates or socialist liberals, and you have the makings of a frightened, financially insecure, self-absorbed and easily manipulated populace that has no energy and attention for understanding and actively participating in political and social life.**

In describing these three strands of the ideology of oppression – that of international politics, of neoliberalism and of the politics of political manipulation – I am not seeking to deny other aspects of disempowerment, such as undermining the rights of women or the equality of African Americans. Nor am I suggesting that all, or even most, political and economic elites would fully subscribe to these beliefs if asked directly, and even less that the general public is aware of, never mind supports, these manipulative values. However, I am convinced that these ideological elements function as unconscious or semi-conscious operating beliefs and values for many elites in capitalistic societies. As Willis Harmon states, 'Collectively held unconscious beliefs shape the world's institutions, and are at the root of institutionalized oppression and inequity'.[22]

Both the neoliberal view of economics and the rules of great power politics have been consciously articulated and are shared by many professionals in economics and international politics, whereas the beliefs undermining genuine democracy are visible but less broadly acknowledged. What these ideologies share is the primacy placed on economic and material life, the emphasis on egotism and self-interest, whether it be that of states, corporations, groups or individuals; and the acceptance of competition, conflict, manipulation and war as viable and preferred strategies for pursuing power and wealth.

What they also justify when seen in tandem is manipulation, lying and corruption; for example the vilification of Rachel Carson by the chemical industry because of her exposure of the dangers of DDT, the denial of the link between cigarettes and cancer by the tobacco industry, and the current opposition to climate change by the oil industry – and, of course, the bribing of politicians and government through financial donations. It is laughable for US lawmakers to criticize other countries for corruption when we treat corporations as persons and allow 'one dollar, one vote'.

That this three-headed ideology inspires policies and actions which threaten the survival of the earth and of societies is increasingly clear. That it has the power of not only undermining other imaginations of our social future but also of shaping our image of what it means to be human, and of what constitutes acceptable behavior, is also evident. It is an ideology of destruction and of the battle of all against all, leading us in the direction of a dystopian future in which the economic, social and political system destroys itself. As Otto Scharmer notes, we now face three divides, or disjunctions: an ecological divide in which we are presently consuming 1.5 times the energy and resource of our planet; a social divide in which just eight billionaires own wealth equal to half the world's population; and a spiritual divide in which 800,000 people commit suicide every year.[23]

While this ideology of oppression has been with us in some form throughout human history, its more modern manifestation has a particular virulence because of the global nature of modern society, and the dominance of technology and the media. I believe in its present form and content it is a response to a shifting mindset in Western society that is moving toward greater psychological and spiritual awareness, a more qualitative ecological and social consciousness, and new principles of structuring society. Harmon described this emerging worldview as 'transmodern', involving a shift in the locus of authority from external to 'inner knowing'. This worldview '...amounts to a reconciliation of scientific inquiry with the perennial philosophy at the core of the world's spiritual traditions'.[24]

The strength and acceptance of this new worldview has been building since the early 1970s of the last century, having pioneered transformations in agriculture, education, alternative medicine and therapy, environmental sustainability, co-operative economics and socially responsible banking. This evolving worldview threatens the ideology of materialism which underlies the other ideologies of oppression and which provides the rationale for the behavior of exploiting the earth and others. It also threatens the older, patriarchial centers of power and control, and so economic, social and political theories are developed and spread which are totally disconnected from this leading edge of human awareness. The debunking of the 1960s as solely a time of hedonism and irresponsibility is part of this defensive strategy.

Many of us are beyond treating nature as an inanimate storehouse to be plundered; we are beyond relying on violence or war as the main way of dealing with disputes; beyond having excess and obscene wealth while poverty and hunger are pervasive; beyond being devoted to consumption as the main source of meaning in life; beyond violent prejudice and hatred; and beyond military style assault weapons being readily available to teenagers. Standing Rock, Black Lives Matter, the Women March in early 2017, the #me Too movement and the recent March for Our Lives – all are beginning to demonstrate a new-found awareness of what has become unacceptable. A substantial part of humanity, especially women and the young, recognizes the sacredness and interdependence of all life forms, and finds the patriarchal, misogynistic nature of the present US administration and aspects of American corporate culture unacceptable.

Humanity has both the knowledge and the capability of designing and creating a more sustainable global economy and a more equitable, non-violent world. Many of the essays in this book point in the direction of viable alternatives: from a basic guaranteed income, the practice of direct democracy and co-operative economics, to seeing safety, health care, education, freedom of speech and association and work as human rights. A new social order based on freedom, equality and a co-operative economy, as an alternative to both socialism and communism, is emerging.

But these changes require that ever-greater numbers of people move from the pursuit of greed and egotism toward a culture of meeting, compassion and of service as a worldview and a practice in life. This implies a painful recognition of the many ways in which the ideology of oppression and also our experiences in modern society, including but not limited to our addiction to the web, separate us from nature, from others and from our better natures. The experiences of separation lead to aliena-tion (the head's inability to comprehend and connect to a complex and rapidly changing world), isolation (the heart's difficulty in connecting to other human beings), and to a sense of powerlessness (the blockage of the will in finding meaningful life activities to contribute to a better world). We become more fearful, lonely individuals, separated from others and the world. Addiction, prejudice and violence are some of the common escapes from these dilemmas, as we become prey to the appeals of our lower nature, and to the lies, manipulations and the seductions of easy answers to complex questions.

So we must do the great work of reconnection, as Joanna Macy calls it, in order to create the experiences for a more meaningful life and a healthier, ecological society.[25] This great work starts with four recognitions: first, that we have lost a living and felt relationship to nature; to the seasons, to the beauty of the night sky and the glory of the first daffodils; secondly, that we have lost a true relationship to others, to the great gifts of conversation, friendship, family life, and the abiding value of partnership and marriage; thirdly, that we are increasingly losing a living connection to our higher self, to our true being which is our guide and inspiration in life; and lastly, that it is within our power to remedy this disconnection and isolation through using the unique gift of modern consciousness, the power of attention.

It is the power of attention which makes the work of reconnection, of genuine relationship, possible, and it is this work which only we can do as individuals.

Notes

1   Martin Luther King, cited in the *New Yorker*, 3 April 2017, 'Martin Luther King's searing anti-war speech; Fifty years later'.

2   See Jacob Needleman, *The American Soul: Rediscovering the Wisdom of the Founders*, Tarcher/Putnam, New York, 2002, p. 19.

3   See the essay 'The Will to Power: The American Empire Project', Chapter 2 in this volume.

4   David Ray Griffin, *Bush and Cheney: How They Ruined America and the World*, Olive Branch Press, Northampton, Mass., 2017. Bush is quoted on p. 23.

5   See the essay 'Disturbing Questions about 9/11 and the War on Terror', Chapter 3 in this volume.

6   'The Crisis of Western Capitalism', Chapter 4 in this volume.

7   See the excellent study by Kevin Phillips, *Bad Money: Reckless Finance, Failed Politics and the Global Financial Crisis*, Penguin, New York, 2008, pp. 2–28.

8   Ryan Vlastelica, *Market Watch*, Friday 5 January 2018.

9   See Ryan Vlastelica, 'Ray Dalio: income inequality is the biggest issue of our time', *Financial News* (London), 26 September 2017; available at goo.gl/cMFJsq (accessed 31 March 2019).

10   David Grinspoon, *Earth in Human Hands: Shaping our Planet's Future*, Grand Central Publishing, New York, 2016, p. xv.

11   Quoted in *The Week*, 17 April 2018. An article in *The Nation*, 2 April 2018 describes Congressman Walter Jones Jr as one of the truly independent voices in the GOP.

12   Griffin, *Bush and Cheney*, op. cit.

13   This verse/saying is attributed to Buddhism as well as to Confucianism. See Quote Investigator.com.

14   Rudolf Steiner, *The Gospel of St John*, Anthroposophic Press, Hudson, New York, 1984, p. 191.

15   Cited in an earlier essay, 'The Will to Power: The American Empire Project', Chapter 2 in this volume.

16   Estimates of the costs for Afghanistan and Iraq vary widely, depending on whether future interest charges and medical costs are included. See Brown University, US 'Budget Costs for Afghanistan and Iraq', September 2016.

17   George Monbiot, 'Neoliberalism: The ideology at the root of all our problems', *The Guardian*, 15 April 2016.

18   See Korten, *When Corporations Rule the World*, op. cit., pp. 70–71.

19   Noam Chomsky, *Requiem for the American Dream: The 10 Principles of Concentration of Wealth and Power*, Seven Stories Press, New York, p. 17.

20   Cited in Chomsky, ibid., p. 124.
21   Chomsky, pp. 151–152.
22   Willis Harmon wrote this wonderful and insightful book in 1988: *Global Mind Change: The Promise of the Last Years of the Twentieth Century*, Knowledge Systems Inc., Indianapolis, Ind., 1988, p. 157.
23   C. Otto Scharmer, *The Essentials of Theory U: Core Principles and Applications*, Berrett-Koehler Publishers, San Francisco, 2017, pp. 4–5.
24   Harmon, *Global Mind Change*, op. cit., p. 27.
25   Joannna Macy and Chris Johnstone, *Active Hope*, op. cit. pp. 6–10.

Chapter 11

Facing Ourselves:
The Work of Reconnection
(October 2018)

The salvation of the human being is through love and in love.

Viktor Frankl

I Attending to Nature

As I sit at my desk on a warm August afternoon I hear the noise of an air-conditioner, the distant sound of a train, and I can notice how the light of the sun cascades over my desk and papers. I can then direct my attention to note the four piles of books sitting on my desk, which I had yesterday told myself to sort and put away. So my consciousness has the power to attend, to shift my attention toward the world around me, toward the sense impressions of the natural and the human world, and at the same time to note what is happening in my mind; I did have the intention to pick up my study yesterday, didn't I? This power of attention and the ability to direct it toward outer or inner phenomena constitute the human extra – it is, I believe, the avenue, the road to overcoming our alienation and isolation. In saying that modern life has eroded our connection to nature, to others and to our deepest and essential self, I am also saying that we have it within our power to remedy this disconnection, to reintegrate ourselves into the world by directing and schooling our consciousness.

By directing our attention to the world of nature we are invited into a world of beauty and wisdom not created by the human being. To see a deer gracefully drinking at the water's edge, or the geese flying north with their urgent cries in March and April, moves me and fills me with delight. I often sit on a bench in our garden and attend to the plants, insects, birds and small animals; the red squirrel scurrying into a hole in the willow tree, the chickadee chattering to me at the feeder or the blue forget-me-nots by the stream with their tiny black centers. Mary Oliver's poetry sometimes helps me to enter this marvelous world in its dialog with the human soul, as do poems by Wendell Berry, W.S. Merwin and Paul Mathews.

> Do the trees speak back to the wind
> When the wind offers some invitational comment?
> As some of us do, do they also talk to the sun?
> I believe so, and if such a belief need rest on
> evidence, let me just say. Sometimes it's
> an earful....[1]

What is it that happens to us when we direct our attention to nature? For me it gives some certainty and hope; the sun will rise in its glory tomorrow morning, the hummingbirds will return from Mexico, and the large blue heron will come in late summer to eat its fill of bullfrogs from our pond.

Nature also generates awe, wonder, gratitude and joy in my soul if I let it, despite my fears about climate change and global warming. These are great gifts to the soul: they build a bridge for me to the certainty of a divine order of which I am part. This does not mean that I dispute the findings of modern science, only that the great ark of the Milky Way and the beauty of a spider web in the morning dew assure me that the world is also ensouled; a living being which I can learn to respect, love and therefore care for.

The living earth manifests wisdom, and reminds me of the cycles of life, of growth and decay, and of the rhythms of day and night and the seasons, all of which are part of me. Paying attention to nature, which I do haphazardly but frequently, also helps me to recognize that I am deeply indebted to plants, animals and minerals for my daily sustenance, that they make my existence possible. Expressing this gratitude has been part of all ancient cultures, and can be brought to modern consciousness by a verse, a prayer or a reflection at mealtime.

The Goethean scientist Craig Holdrege notes the many ways in which Nature can also be our teacher, if we attend to it and seek to understand it:

> One could hardly imagine a better teacher of dynamism, connectedness, resilience, and wholeness than the plant. The plant shows us how to

live in transformation; it shows us context sensitivity, it shows us the unique nature of organisms; it shows us how to overcome an object-relation to the world. By developing a thinking modeled after such characteristics, our thinking becomes fluid and dynamic; we realize how we are embedded in the world; we become sensitive and responsive to the contexts we meet in the world and we learn to thrive in a changing world.[2]

By attending to the natural world we overcome something of our alienation and isolation, we learn more about a living thinking, and we learn about principles of interdependence and mutual service, principles of great importance for the human and social world.

Walking in nature and perceiving what is taking place also makes us sensitive to the perils of industrial agriculture, the damage caused by pollution, and the shift in weather patterns due to global warming, and it awakens the heart to becoming a more responsible steward of the earth. Plant a flower bed, tend a garden, keep a beehive, pick fresh raspberries or admire the sunset, and you will feel more connected, integrated, more whole and somehow more human. As Rachel Carson once remarked to a group of women journalists after the publication of her first successful book, *The Sea Around Us*, 'The more clearly we can focus our attention on the wonders and realities of the universe about us, the less taste we shall have for destruction'.[3]

II Meeting the Other and Healing the World

In addition to reconnecting to nature we can bring our attention to practicing genuine conversation and true human encounter. We are conceived in relationship, we are born into the relationships of family, we are nurtured and educated in relationship, we find our calling and our life in relationship, and as human beings, we create the social world in dialogue with others, in relationship. Human meeting and conversation are truly the central, archetypal phenomena of all social life. By focusing our attention on our dialogue with others, on the practice of deep listening, we can find the keys to working on ourselves, to building relationships and to healing society.

It is meaningful and open conversation which enlivens, builds empathy, bridges divides, strengthens community and makes social action possible. As Sherry Turkle states in *Reclaiming Conversation*, being fully present to each other, we learn to listen. It's where we develop the capacity for empathy. It's where we experience the joy of being heard, of being understood. And conversation advances self-reflection, the conversations with ourselves that are the cornerstones of early development and continue throughout life.[4]

Because conversation and meeting are so taken for granted and so commonplace in our life, we don't notice and bring to awareness what actually happens in human encounter, largely sleeping through the experiences which are capable of transforming our understanding and experience of social life. Uncovering this blind spot in human encounter requires reflexively bringing to consciousness that which happens when two or more human beings meet, converse and build relationship.

Conversation and Encounter: Lessons for Social Transformation

It is in and through my 'knowing the kind of person you are and you knowing the kind of person I am', as William Stafford suggests in his poem, 'A Ritual to Read to Each Other', that we can heal ourselves and build healthier communities and a more caring society.[5] The lessons from human meetings and conversations at home and at work that I try to bring to awareness and ask you to consider and explore include:

I and You

I have self-consciousness, an I, which gives me the power of attention which I can direct both at you in listening and at my own soul experiences when meeting with others. And so can you. This reflective I-consciousness allows me to monitor what happens in my soul in the process of speaking and listening, of meeting with others. I experience an I and a you, both of us beings of body, soul and spirit engaged in dialogue. In this dialogue we are sharing thoughts, feelings and intentions, turning something intangible and interior into audible, sensory speech, and in listening, turning these sounds into understanding. So we are speaking, listening and understanding, and in the process discovering our individuality, our relationship and our humanity as social beings.

Social and Anti-Social Forces

When directing my attention at what I experience in meeting others, I discover both social and anti-social qualities living within me. In listening intently, I realize that I am letting the other into my soul and am awake to them, their ideas and wishes, and more asleep to my own thoughts and reactions. I can stretch out this listening and being open and interested in time, although it requires an effort to stay open and not to assert myself, saying 'well, have you thought of, or yes, but'. I also realize that with friends and in relationships of trust, I can frequently listen longer and with empathy and encouragement for the speaker. I then have both an open mind and an open heart, manifesting interest and empathy toward the other. These are important social forces which I am able to exercise in trusting and creative social circumstances. Having had that experience and the resulting feelings of joy and creativity, I can then practice extending them to conversations that are more problematic. This requires an effort to stop my reactive self, my defensive responses.

Here, I am reminded of a dyad exercise to which a dear friend introduced me, and which I have sometimes used to create a mood of deep listening in groups that I have worked with because it suspends our more anti-social sides for a brief period of time. Two people sit across from each other and ask who are you, each sharing for five minutes without interruption, and then the speaker asks the listener the same question. Once you have done this two or three times each, you realize what a relief to have such a space of listening and of interest, and also how much of yourself you have shared in such a short time. Sharing particular biographical questions serves a similar function: describe the girl you were at six, who helped and advised you in college; share an experience which led to your present work or how you met your beloved. By being interested in the other and by listening, we discover the miracle of mutual understanding, of empathy, of meeting, and we recognize that we are all brothers and sisters on the journey of life, a journey full of hopes, dreams, tragedies and triumphs. Once we have this experience with the other, an important bond is formed, deeper friendship is possible, and a circle of trust is created.

We can also notice anti-social forces working in us, the doubts and skepticism which we find in our thinking life as we listen to others, the likes and dislikes in our feelings, and the egotism in wanting our way. These tendencies don't require effort. They are the residue, the by-product of modern society and a central characteristic of modern consciousness. They help us to know what we think, feel and want, they give us a sense of self and at the same time they cut us off from others. It is these forces, together with the ever-present media devices, which help to create the epidemic of loneliness in Western societies and the empathy deficit which researchers are noting amongst our young people.[6]

As I bring these anti-social forces to my awareness, through paying attention to what is happening within me during conversation, I realize that the very problems and issues I have been describing previously – an economy geared to self and the survival of the fittest, or a politics based on exploitation, prejudice and manipulation and a mindset of cynicism and oppression – each have their home in me, as well as in the world. The anti-social forces which underlie the ideology of oppression are also ours: egotism, cynicism, greed, prejudice and even hatred of the other. They give us our self-awareness, but when not balanced by more conscious caring relationships – by friendship and community – they lead in the direction of an ego-centered, oppressive and often violent society.

Transforming Shadow in Self and World

It is in and through our relationship with others, through our colleagues, friends and our partners and children that we become most aware of our anti-social sides, and also of our individual shadow. They point out to us that we have stopped listening, that we have not been honest, that we have manipulated and lied, or that we harbor prejudice. It is out of our relationship to others that the need for working on ourselves is made most visible, and often with an urgency that is hard to deny.

In my experience it is often in conflict situations that our darker, untransformed sides are shown to ourselves and to the world most clearly. It is in such situations that we also become aware of three levels of response to other people. We have perceptions of the other which can lead to fixed images: 'Mary is always late, or Mexicans are unreliable, or men are so one-dimensional'. These perceptions lead to attitudes and feelings; likes and dislikes, annoyance, anger, and these in turn inform behavior; automatic assent or dissent, avoidance, silence, shouting, and in some cases to violence.

Conflicts usually start with an incident or a misunderstanding that can easily escalate to argument and mutual criticism, to a hardening of perceptions and attitudes which then leads to alliance building, a simplification of issues and selective memory, and then perhaps to threats and counter-threats and eventually to violence and war. We have all been on this ladder, harboring grudges, planning arguments or actions to undermine the other. And we unfortunately see this pattern at work in the world too frequently, between the Buddhist majority and the Rohingha in Myanmar, between Palestinians and Israelis at the Gaza border, between white nationalists in northern Europe and the newly arriving Muslim refugees from Syria, Iraq or Afghanistan. And, of course, we see it in our own society in the pattern of race relations or increasingly in attitudes of Democrats and Republicans toward each other, particularly during this time of the Trump administration.

We lose both ourselves and the other in conflicts. In ourselves we can notice hot anger and aggression as well as a colder desire to hurt or damage the other, and we say things and act in ways that later can make us ashamed. As to the other person or other parties, we end up demonizing them, losing all perspective and the understanding that they, too, are human, and want the same things that we do – freedom of expression and the right to be treated as equal human beings.

In my experience, becoming aware of and struggling to transform my lower self, made visible to me in relationships, but in particular through conflicts, has three distinct benefits. First, it makes me aware of the need for inner work and perhaps for counseling and therapy; secondly, it sharpens my sense of social and political discernment, making me less susceptible to manipulation by others and the media; and thirdly, it awakens a desire to become a more caring and loving person. Thus, consciousness of our shadow, our untransformed self, offers us a great service if we are willing to acknowledge it, and work to transform it.

Working on ourselves can happen in many ways, through Alcoholics Anonymous and mutual support groups, through friendship, biography work, counseling, artistic work, self-reflection, and to being engaged with one of the great spiritual and religious traditions of humanity in the quest for spiritual and moral development. To not do such work and to not acknowledge the gap between who we are in part and what we are becoming is to fall into the morass of lying, false accusations, projections and total self-absorption which is so often visible in our politics. It is to become a victim of our double as a person and a society. As Gandhi said many years ago, in what is certainly an overstatement, but one which carries an essential truth, 'The only devils in the world... are those running around in our own souls. That is where the battle should be fought.'[7]

The Heart's Journey
It is through human relationships that our anti-social and untransformed shadow nature becomes visible to us. Others become *the mirror* to us for that which needs to be acknowledged and worked on in ourselves. The *invitation* which others and which conflict situations provide is to transform judgement and dislike into interest in the other which, if genuine, can lead to understanding and empathy, and to a process of healing.

In doing interpersonal conflict resolution work I have found it important to help bring perceptions and mutual attitudes to consciousness and, above all, to provide opportunities for the parties to share aspects of their life story. For in conflict situations we invariably lose the humanity of the other, and the best way of overcoming this is to share our stories.

I am on the Board of the Karuna Center for Peacebuilding in Amherst, Mass., and am deeply moved and humbled by their work in Rwanda and other war-torn societies in which genocide has occurred. It is hard to imagine a Tutsi mother talking to, never mind holding the hand of, a Hutu perpetrator, and yet this happens. The power of the heart to hate is great, but the heart's capacity to forgive is even greater. This is what peace and reconciliation processes in Rwanda, South Africa, Sri Lanka and other nations make possible. In a small way it is what Story Corp in New York, referred to earlier, is beginning to offer to friends and family members divided by politics and ideology in One Step at a Time, a listening booth and common questions to explore together in a neutral and safe space.

The journey from interest to empathy to compassion and love is the heart's journey. It is easier with our children, grandchildren and friends, and harder with people who are different than we are, or who come from other nations, cultures or races. Yet this is the journey which relation-ships offer, and which the practice of genuine listening makes possible. It is what makes bridging the gap between ourselves and others not only possible but worth the effort, because we recognize that we are brothers and sisters on the road of mutual development, that we need each other to be whole.

Life Partnership and Family Life
There is no greater opportunity for practicing interest, empathy and love than in the family. It is here that we are truly challenged to becoming loving human beings, and where we have the opportunity to develop life-long relationships. It is here that we can witness the development of our children from innocent helpless beings to toddlers, to demanding seven year-olds and to unique and sometimes outrageous teenagers. We experi-ence the evolution of children as individualities, often mirroring back to us our own foibles and inconsistencies. We are asked to be their wardens and trustees, helping them to find their future, not ours. This asks for sensitivity and tenderness as well as a deep perception and interest in whom they are becoming. And we have to be willing to let them make mistakes and to provide them with the resources, financial and otherwise, for their life journey. This is a tall order, even for a couple in a stable rela-tionship, never mind a single parent.

Then there is the challenge of partnership and marriage itself. I often think mutual attraction is a ruse to bring us together in order to have us work on our relationships over time, to learn to love another over years, with all of our differences of personality, gender, temperament and orientation. It is hard work, involving compromise, honesty and a willingness to help each other grow through challenge and adversity. Women are more apt to recognize that relationships require tending than men, who may feel less adept at sorting out feelings, never mind sharing them. As a man in a marriage for many decades, with two children and two grandchildren, I have learned to deeply appreciate the conversational and relationship skills of women and their ability to share themselves. I used to think how is it that they can talk so much and for so long with each other, but I have come to see that their abundance of sharing is the asset of a more feminine, life-enhancing consciousness, which I can learn from and seek to cultivate, and which our overly masculine culture badly needs.

If partnership and family constitute the great practice ground for social reform, as I believe they are, then it is here that we can practice developing a healthier set of human relationships, a new society. If we believe in the freedom of the individual, do we grant our partner the right to have different opinions, different values, different interests and even to belong to another religion? As our children grow into adolescence and young adulthood, do we encourage them to develop their own friendships and their particular interests, and do we converse with them about moral and ethical standards? At the dinner table, do we have conversation at all by shutting off our TV and other devices in order to have a free dialogue about the events of the day?

In the realm of economics, our co-operative family economy, we have always had joint checking and savings accounts as a couple, and have worked with the principle of 'From each according to their ability, and to each according to their need', in pooling income and in deciding on priorities in spending; saving money on cars and clothes, and spending more on travel, books and education for ourselves and our children. Money has not been used between us or with our children as a carrot or a stick. When we can, we help children and grandchildren financially, and have discussed our will with both of our children, always seeking to treat them equally.

Loving others is hard, and as a couple we have had troubled times and heartbreak. We have also had explosive moments with our children and serious disagreements, but we have stayed in dialogue and in relationship, respecting each other and loving each other on our different life journeys.

Friendship

I have a small number of good friends, some far away, and others fortunately close by. When we meet it is as if we help each other to bloom, to come to our truer selves and somehow to be fuller and more whole. In listening to the eco-biologist Andreas Weber recently, I realized that he used three words and concepts which describe essential elements of true relationship for me: the relationship is mutually transformative, it is reciprocal, and it generates aliveness in all parties. This is true of our relationship to nature and also true of human friendship.

In reflecting on experiences of friendship, I remembered a book by Laurens van der Post titled *Jung and the Story of Our Time,* in which he describes his long conversations with Carl Jung in Jung's book-lined study outside of Zurich. He describes an experience we all have in important friendships:

> What was of overwhelming consequence to me was that as we sat there talking, something was communicated to me of what Jung was in himself, rather than out of his ideas. In this process the feeling of isolation and loneliness in a vital area of myself, which had haunted me all those years, vanished. I was no longer alone. I had company of a noble order.[8]

We can all become company of a noble order to others by practicing listening and pursuing the path of interest, empathy and compassion, in consciously developing friendships. And in so doing we also contribute to a healthier and more satisfying old age, as multiple studies have shown.

Witnessing our Times

Developing interest in the other, listening, and developing empathy and compassion also build the capacity to be an active witness to what is happening in the world. Listening requires that we still our mind and hearts, that we pay attention to the other. The same is true of witnessing what is happening around us, and what the media presents to us as news. To be an active citizen is to pay attention to issues and questions over time, to be discerning about the information we let into our soul, as described in the earlier essay titled 'Witnessing the Long Emergency' (Chapter 1). By paying attention to the other in conversation, we gain insight and we open our hearts, developing empathy for others and for the plight of the world and the seemingly endless circumstances of human struggle and suffering. This can ignite in us the desire to help the other and to do good in the world, to join others in the struggle for peace, greater justice and community.

I have previously described three interconnected activities in witnessing our times as the path of insight, the journey of compassion and the path of will and transformation. They can also be described more simply as developing an open mind, an open heart and an open will, as Otto Scharmer does in his Presencing work. They follow and emerge from being interested in the other, developing understanding and empathy for the other, and wanting to help and serve the other. This is what we can practice in relationship, in friendship, in our family, neighborhood, and places of work, thereby building the capacity to be active witnesses and participants in the struggle to build a better world. This struggle is never over, either in ourselves or in the world, and yet it is one of the things which gives our life meaning and purpose, for it invites us to overcome our egotism and isolation, to engage in building 'beloved community', which is what made the civil-rights movement such a powerful force for good in the lives of so many Americans.

Awakening the Forces of Social Renewal

What makes deep friendship and love between people such a powerful force for good is that it also can awaken the soul forces of social reform in us: it can awaken the heart's longing for freedom, equality, and sisterhood and brotherhood. In conversation with good friends, with close working partners and with my wife, adult children, and grandchildren and in meaningful encounters of all kinds, I experience a desire to learn, to be open, to respect the other's freedom. If I sense that the other has an agenda or is not interested in listening, I withdraw and wait or fall into arguing myself, in which case neither is respecting the freedom and independence of the other. If one of us is dominating, is taking too much space and time by talking too much and with too much energy, we also feel slighted as not only is our sense of freedom, of our individual uniqueness, violated, but so is our sense of fairness, of equity. Being a talker myself, I am very aware of the temptation to monopolize, and have had to learn to hold back to listen to the other, to safeguard both their freedom and their sense of equity. Research has shown that what distinguishes effective working groups and conversations from those that are less effective is the rough equality of participation. If I can be interested in the other, and be delighted by their uniqueness, respecting their freedom of thought and grant them equality, parity of participation as well as experiencing their striving evolving human self, then I want to help, to support, and achieve mutual understanding and creativity.

It is through my relationship to others that I awaken to my deep soul longing for personal freedom and responsibility, my desire to be seen and treated as an equal citizen of the world, to have a say in my life and work, and to find meaning and purpose through giving and serving others. This longing and desire is an intrinsic part of being human, which while awakened through relationships can also be masked and undermined by the media, by addictions and by the ideology of oppression, that turns life for many people into a struggle for survival, and work into a kind of slavery. Once awakened in us, this longing to experience our full humanity as free, equal and mutually embedded in community can become our beacon for social reform. If I am right, and this threefold experience is truly the expression of our heart's longing, as it was in the French Revolution with its call for freedom, equality and fraternity, then it leads us away from the old and, by now, sterile arguments between left and right. Instead of arguing about more or less government, we can ask how educational and cultural life can foster our freedom as sovereign individuals, how political and state life can guarantee our equality before the law and in social life, and what an economy truly serving human needs and the earth would look like.

Recognizing Our Mutual Indebtedness
It is through others that we find ourselves. We learn language through family and friends, we experience love through others, we develop through the help of teachers, mentors and colleagues, and we eat, clothe and find shelter and work through what others have provided. We are predominately social beings and serve each other through what Kropotkin called Mutual Aid, and what Martin Luther King expressed as the network of mutuality:

> All men are caught in an inescapable network of mutuality, tied in a single garment of destiny. I can never be what I ought to be until you are what you ought to be and you can never be what you ought to be until I am what I ought to be.[9]

It is through becoming aware of our relationship to others, through dialog and encounter, that we can recognize our mutual indebtedness, and develop deep gratitude for others and the social world. This in turn awakens a sense for the thread of destiny, of intentionality, purpose and guidance in our life. And it fires our will to serve others and the future. Consider the question of which people, colleagues, teachers and friends have opened important doors for you in becoming who you are today, and also for whom you have been the inspiration for new steps in their life. You will marvel at the synchronicity of life.

Intentionality and the Question of Karma

I have long had a sense that life is intentional, meaning that it is not just random chance that I met an important teacher and mentor when I was 28 at a youth conference in 1970 that changed my life. Nor that I was involved in a gun accident with my father at 13 that had a deep impact on me, nor that I encountered my beloved through mutual friends in a rather bizarre sequence of events in my middle 20s. I have a feeling that our life has a fundamental design to it, a life pattern in which we are challenged to work with certain themes and questions as opportunities for learning and for growth.

Given the multiple similar accounts of near-death experiences and the continuity of consciousness, is it so far-fetched to think that we have a spiritual kernel which incarnates as an I, sometimes as a man and sometimes as a women over the course of time in order to become a wiser, more loving being. Rudolf Steiner gives a picture that after we cast off our physical body in death, we review our life as others and the world have experienced us, from the outside in, so to speak, and that out of this profound and at times painful review we distill the lessons for our future incarnation.[10]

While there is no conclusive proof of the reality of reincarnation and karma, there is a growing body of personal and empirical evidence to support it. Some years ago I ran across two interesting and compelling books: *Old Souls: The Scientific Evidence for Past Lives* by Tom Schroeder, which examines the highly detailed research of Dr Ian Stevenson into the thousands of young children's recollections of previous incarnations; and *Expecting Adam* by Martha Beck, in which she recounts her inner experiences in dialogue with her still-to-be-born son.[11]

Bringing the perspective of intentionality into our life experiences, that we are each in some sense the authors of our biography, leads to asking questions of meaning and potential learning. Why am I a women or a Chinese American; what did I intend to learn from being an only child; what has been the gift of my struggle with cancer? The perspective of a self-intended destiny and of reincarnation can be empowering and helpful, moving us from blaming and victimhood into the search for understanding and meaning. It is, I think, a profound source of hope; we can learn to set this right, we can deepen our understanding and we can become a better person.

Over 25 per cent of the American public has a sense for the reality of karma and reincarnation, according to the Pew Forum on Religion and Public Life.[12] What would it mean for social life if we deepened our sensitivity to this reality, were awake to important karmic moments, and began to experience the threads of karma as the reality which held our lives and that of the social world together?

Working with Others

We live and work in families and groups. The lessons for social transformation can best be practiced here, as I have suggested. This is where listening and building authentic relationships become most real, where reconciling differences and conflicts becomes essential, and where practicing the principles of a new, freer and more sharing society is possible. It is here that a new crucible for democracy and a new society is emerging, as millions of groups in civil society around the world engage in the great experiment of building conscious relationships and community in order to build a better world. They are working with techniques of conscious dialogue, with Non-Violent Communication, with Consensus Decision-making and Sociocracy, and are creating both learning but also resource-sharing communities.

In the late 1990s the Fetzer Institute and the Institute of Noetic Science sponsored a study and a series of conferences on the theme of group synergy and collective intelligence. The conditions for joint creativity which they identified included:

- A joint commitment to each other and a clear and shared human and spiritual purpose.
- Developing an atmosphere of safety, confidentiality, trust and respect.
- Speaking from the heart and out of experience.
- Inclusivity and respect toward different human and spiritual orientations.
- A willingness to play.
- An ability to deal with differences and with conflict.
- Creating a sacred space open to guidance and inspiration.
- A joint commitment to inner development and learning.
- A meeting that is prepared, held and guided by a clear process and form of facilitation.[13]

It is when we grant each other freedom of thought and expression, offer mutual understanding and empathy based on equality, and have a shared desire to achieve a mutually beneficial outcome, that magic happens, and we realize an unexpected creativity and depth of conversation. It is as if a good spirit provides inspiration and guidance, and we feel enlivened, seen and trusted, and desire to contribute to healing in the world. It is an experience which nourishes the soul and engenders energy, hope, compassion and love.

III Reconnecting to Spirit: The Practice of Inner Development

Reconnecting to the beauty and gifts of nature helps us to learn gratitude and reverence for life, and opens us to the experience and understanding of the earth as a living being. It also leads us from seeking to use and exploit the earth to becoming stewards of the earth, in both larger and smaller ways. Focusing our attention on the nature of human encounter, on human relationships and conversation, reveals our indebtedness to others, on the challenge of overcoming our egotism, and transforming our anti-social sides so that we may become more caring and loving human beings.

The inevitable confrontation with our shadow sides through human encounter also reveals the necessity for working on ourselves if we are attentive and honest. It raises questions of good and evil, of the moral compass of life, and offers us the challenge of self-development and transformation. I think there is no better door to a more just world than through answering the call, sounded so long ago in the ancient mysteries – 'Oh human being, know yourself!'. This call is also carried in the very idea of America, as Jacob Needleman noted in his study, *The American Soul*:

> The meaning of democracy was always rooted in a vision of human nature as both fallen and perfectible – inwardly fallen and inwardly perfectible. To a significant extent, democracy in its specifically American form was created to allow men and women to seek their own higher principle within themselves. Without that inner meaning, democracy becomes, …a celebration of disorder and superficiality.[14]

When I mention a self-chosen path of inner development, I mean a path which shares basic principles found in all spiritual traditions. Whether Christian, Buddhist, Hindu, Jewish or Muslim, the great spiritual and religious traditions of humanity share three essential qualities. The first of these is reverence and gratitude for the earth and the miracle of life; the second could be called the practice of mindfulness, of educating the soul to bring greater consciousness to outer and inner experiences; while the third quality is a dialogue with the divine, with the spiritual world, through prayer and meditation.

Practicing reverence and gratitude establishes a basic soul mood essential for connecting us to life and the world around us. Rudolf Steiner remarked, 'We advance ever more quickly (on the path of inner development), if in such moments (of inner reflection), we fill our consciousness with admiration, respect and reverence for the world and for life'.[15] To cultivate this mood of reverence we need to attend... – to attend to a young child giggling with a friend, to the rain refreshing a small pond, or to the poet's or musician's voice. Above all, we need moments of quiet reflection, no I-phone or computer screen, in order to ponder our life and to learn to hear our inner voice.

Mindfulness activities are exercises to educate and direct our soul faculties of thinking, feeling and willing so that we enhance our capacities to experience the world and ourselves more consciously. Attending to different dimensions of nature; studying cloud and weather patterns, observing insect and animal life are mindfulness activities, as is attending to what happens inside me when I am in a difficult conversation with a colleague or a partner.

We all have the experience of beginning to think about a question – say, a meeting with a friend about a Board meeting two weeks from now – and before we know it, we are thinking about an upcoming dental bill, or whether the car needs an oil change. It is the same with our feelings: someone makes a flippant remark about a mutual friend, and we react with annoyance and stay out of sorts through the rest of the conversation; or we hear someone make a political remark, which in principle we agree with, but decide to query it because there is something about the person we don't like, without really knowing why. Sometimes things go deeper still. My grand-daughter, whom I love dearly, is a picky eater, to which I used to react a bit harshly, until my wife asked me why this bothered me so; and I realized that it was because as a young boy I experienced hunger after the Second World War. Bringing this to consciousness helped me to achieve more equanimity when she asked for special dishes at the local restaurant.

In the area of our will, things are still more precarious in following our conscious intentions. I start upstairs to sign some fund-raising letters and notice a copy of a magazine on the stairs which I pick up and begin reading, forgetting what I intended to do. Or in order to lose a few pounds, I promised myself to stop my mid-night snacking and yet I find myself having a jam sandwich at 11 p.m. the next night. If I add to that food, tobacco, alcohol, drug and internet addictions, from which many of us suffer in some form, we each face the question of to what degree are we thought, felt and willed by outer circumstances or have some measure of control and self-direction? Mindfullness activities, as inner work, can help us become more aware of these intrusions, and lead us to experience the world more fully.

The eight-fold path of the Buddha describes a well-established path of mindfulness exercises. These include: *Right Judgement*, to uncover and bring to consciousness the reasons and motives for a decision or action; *Right Word*, bringing thoughtfulness to our speech and conversation; *Right Deed*, bringing to awareness the consequences of our actions before taking them; *Right Standpoint*, assessing our position in regard to the truths of life; *Right Endeavor*, to devote energy and effort to moral and just causes; *Right Memory*, the effort to learn as much as possible from life through conscious reflection; *Right Opinion*, paying attention to one's thinking, and distinguishing between the essential and non-essential in the search for truth; *Right Examination* – in moments of inner quiet, to take counsel with oneself to form and test the principles of one's life; and lastly, to let these exercises Become a Habit in daily life.[16] The Buddha gave the eight-fold path as a set of practices to his disciples and to humanity as part of his teachings on love and compassion, as a way of overcoming the pain and suffering of the world.

For Rudolf Steiner, there were certain conditions which needed to be met for a path of inner development to be healthy and grounded in the realities of life. He suggested practicing clear thinking, focused will, fostering equanimity in our feeling life, positivity and open-mindedness as well as balancing these soul practices throughout our life.

The first, *control of thinking*, involves placing an ordinary object in your consciousness – say, a button or paperclip – preferably human-made, and focusing on it exclusively for five minutes or more. What is its function, of what and how is it made, and how is it manufactured and sold? Do this for a week or more, and then *add a will exercise* – for example, at 3.30 every day to turn your ring, or to take off your left shoe. A meaningless activity, except that it is difficult to remember to do it at the time you chose.

The practice of equanimity is recommended next so that we are not too strongly affected by ordinary events, moved to great fluctuations of joy or sorrow, and are able to sense what our feelings are conveying to us.

The fourth exercise involves *developing positivity*, seeing the good and the positive in events and in the world, without denying that which is difficult or ugly. The practice of positivity is subtle, for it asks us to move behind our automatic likes and dislikes and see situations in a broader context. *Open-mindedness*, the fifth activity, is a growing challenge as we grow older and are weighed down by both knowledge and experience, as well as being set in our ways.

Working with these five exercises, two asking for set times of practice and the other three in the course of the day, we then seek to *integrate them into our daily consciousness* as the sixth activity.[17]

While mindfulness exercises vary between individuals and across different spiritual traditions, they share the aim of educating awareness. Working with a small group of students some years ago on questions of inner development, I noted over 40 different practices they were engaged in, from conscious walking to toning, to deep breathing, nature observation, a review of the day before sleep, conscious listening and weather observation.

By working on our soul development through mindfulness activities, we prepare the ground for prayer and meditation as complementary ways of addressing the spirit. Prayer is fundamentally 'an upward gaze of the soul from the transitory present into the eternal that embraces past, present and future'.[18] It is a cry to the divine to fill us with its spirit. Whatever its form and irrespective of religious tradition, true prayer leads to a recognition that we are all connected, part of the divine world and recognize a power and a wisdom beyond intellectual knowing. We seek comfort in the lap of the divine to which our will is subservient, whether Allah, Krishna, Buddha or Christ.

If prayer is a petition to the divine world to be present in our life, then meditation is an effort to raise our consciousness to the spiritual world through non-material images, verses and the contemplation of eternal truths, often first articulated by sages, spiritual teachers and saints, and carried in sacred texts. In meditating on the profound phrase from the St John's Gospel, 'In the beginning was the Word and the Word was with God and the Word was God', or the Hindu saying, 'Man habitually identifies the self with the non-self', we are seeking to elevate our consciousness to a spirit beholding. In so doing we develop an awareness that we are a spiritual as well as an earthly being, with the capacity to gain wisdom and love. Having even a small experience of spirit presence creates awe, gratitude and humility, and a deep longing for more of this connection. Arthur Zajonc calls this experience 'the birth of the silent self'. It can be seen as developing a living connection to our true spiritual core.[19]

There are many individual ways of meditating and different established meditation traditions. A friend of mine worked with the Beatitudes of the Sermon on the Mount daily for over 30 years, and used it as a guide in all of his business dealings. Other friends go to week-long meditation retreats based on the Sufi tradition of Islam, while still others participate regularly in zazen Buddhist group meditations or in meditation retreats based on the Western esoteric tradition of Rudolf Steiner.

When we consciously begin our inner journey, one of the first things we meet is our double, the shadow side of our nature, expressing itself in fear, anger, inner laziness, greed and a host of other unattractive qualities. As described earlier, it is usually our partners, children and colleagues who make such qualities visible to us, often painfully. Yet going on an inner journey also gives us the strength to listen to that which others and the world reveal to us, leading us to acknowledge that we are each mighty, beautiful and creative beings, while at the same time being drawn to the dark, and manifesting tragic flaws.

In his reflections on *Owning Your own Shadow*, Robert Johnson describes the human being as standing on a seesaw, trying to balance the forces of light and the dark.[20] Such a balance was ritualistically achieved in the Catholic Mass, with its demons and angels, and also in confession, where the deeds of the shadow were acknowledged and atoned for through penance and prayer. The search for balance was also embodied in the rituals of indigenous peoples and in Hindu and Buddhist festivals. Today, these rituals and practices have lost their meaning and power, and we are left to find our own way in relating to, and honoring, the different sides of our being.

Acknowledging the dual nature of our being, which the world and especially our relationships reveal to us, is a beginning. Sensing what these forces want, are telling us about ourselves and the world is a further step. By using our power of attention in closely following what is occurring within us and around us, we can slow down our more automatic reactions of anger, projection, fear, violence and greed. We can even name and give an image to those aspects of our double which frequently beset us like demons. In psychotherapy, such work can involve having a dialogue with our sub-personalities, and within the Jungian tradition to find ways of acknowledging our shadow through ceremony and ritual.

In my experience, the shadow often works with the force of fear, in particular the fear of being unworthy, of not being good enough. As a result, we become invested in that reality, acting in ways to fulfill the message, sabotaging who we actually are and limiting our opportunities for realizing our potential.

Certainly, the shadow, or double, is a great mystery. It is centrally connected to the questions of good and evil in history and in our time. Going on a path of inner development gives us the strength to recognize the shadow elements in our being, to develop some humility about ourselves, and to ask for help from the human and divine world in transforming ourselves. I think that Robert Johnson is right when he writes:

> Any repair of our fractured world must start with individuals who have the insight and the courage to own their own shadow. Nothing out there will help if the interior projecting mechanism of humankind is operating strongly. The tendency to see one's shadow out there, in one's neighbor or in another race or culture is the most dangerous aspect of the modern psyche.[21]

I have argued that by building a living relationship to nature, the ground of our existence, to other human beings and to community, the social world through which we become human and find our meaning and purpose in life, and to the divine and spiritual worlds, which is the source of our true creativity, we become more caring and loving beings, and become more able to do good in the world. Of course argument and persuasion are not enough. We need to do the work, individually and together. It is as Vaclav Havel says:

> It is I who must begin,
> Once I begin, once I try –
> Here and now....
> To live in harmony
> With 'the voice of Being' as I
> understand it within myself
> – as soon as I begin that
> I suddenly discover,
> To my surprise, that
> I am neither the only one,
> nor the first, ...
> Whether all is really lost
> or not depends entirely on
> whether or not I am lost.[22]

Notes

1   Mary Oliver, *Felicity: Poems*, Penguin Press, New York, 2016, p. 13.
2   Craig Holdrege, *Thinking Like a Plant: A Living Science for Life*, Steiner Books, Great Barrington, Mass., 2013, p. 10.
3   Andrea Barnet, *Visionary Women: How Rachel Carson, Jane Jacobs, Jane Goodall and Alice Waters Changed Our World*, Harper Collins, New York, 2018, p. 63.
4   Sherry Terkle, *Reclaiming Conversation: The Power of Talk in the Digital Age*, Penguin Press, New York, 2015, p. 3.
5   William E. Stafford, available online at goo.gl/gSHrJL (accessed 1 April 2019).
6   'The epidemic of loneliness', *New York Times*, 5 September 2016.
7   Gandhi, quoted in Jerimiah Abrams, *The Shadow in America*, op. cit., p. 41.
8   Laurens van der Post, *Jung and the Story of Our Time*, Hogarth Press, London, 1976, p. 55.
9   Martin Luther King Jr, quoted from *A Letter from Birmingham Jail*, in *The Atlantic*, April 2013.
10 Rudolf Steiner, *Reincarnation and Karma: Two Fundamental Truths of Human Existence*, Steiner Press, Great Barrington, Mass., 1992, pp. 62–82.
11 Tom Schroeder, *Old Souls: The Scientific Evidence for Past Lives*, Simon and Schuster, New York, 1999. Martha Beck, *Expecting Adam: A True Story of Birth, Rebirth and Everyday Magic*, Random House, New York, 2000.
12 Pew Charitable Trust, *Pew Forum on Religion and Public Life*, 2016.
13 Fetzer Institute, Robert Kenny, *Group Service and Group Synergy*, Kalamazoo, Miss., 2000.
14 Jacob Needleman, *The American Soul*, op. cit., p. 10.
15 Rudolf Steiner, *How to Know Higher Worlds*, Steiner Press, Great Barrington, Mass., 1996, p. 20.
16 Walpole Sri Rahula, 'The Noble Eightfold Path', Tricycle.com.
17 Rudolf Steiner, *Guidance in Esoteric Training*, Rudolf Steiner Press, London, 1977, pp. 13–19.
18 Steiner, ibid.
19 Arthur Zajonc, *Meditation as Contemplative Inquiry*, Steiner Press, Great Barrington, Mass., 2009, pp. 30–32.
20 Robert Johnson, *Owning Your Own Shadow: Understanding the Dark Side of the Psyche*, Harper-Collins, New York, 1991, p. 9.
21 Johnson, pp. 14–16.
22 Vaclav Havel, 'It is I who must begin', available at www.kosmosjournal.org/news/poem-it-is-i-who-must-begin-by-vaclav-havel/ (accessed 1 April 2019).

Chapter 12

Re-imagining America:
Building Communities of Conscience
(February 2019)

America is the fact, the symbol and the promise of a new beginning.

Jacob Needleman

As I ponder our future as a society and a people, I have a heavy heart because of the recent tragic murders (as I write) of Jewish worshippers at the Tree of Life synagogue in Pittsburgh, the mailings of pipe bombs to prominent Democrats by Cesar Sayoc, and the senseless slaying of two elderly African Americans in Virginia. Historically, xenophobia, racism and anti-semitism have been the poisons which have most effectively undermined democracies and prepared the way for authoritarian regimes. We are a divided nation, with a president who endlessly stokes such divisions, while attacking the press and the idea of public truth.

America was founded on three central political ideas, 'these truths', as Thomas Jefferson called them: the idea of political and legal equality for human beings; of natural rights, including life, liberty and the pursuit of happiness; and of the popular sovereignty of the people, the consent of the governed. These ideals were a mighty call not only to the citizens of the United States but to people from around the world seeking a better life. Yet from the very beginning and throughout our history we have lived with profound contradictions. As Lepore notes in her recent history of the USA:

A nation born in revolution will forever struggle against chaos. A nation founded on universal rights will wrestle against the forces of particularism. A nation that toppled a hierarchy of birth only to erect a hierarchy of wealth will never know tranquility. A nation of immigrants cannot close its borders. And a nation born in contradiction, liberty in a land of slavery, sovereignty in a land of conquest, will fight, forever, over the meaning of its history.[1]

The question we face, then, is whether we can accept that our history is one of both high aspirations and noble truths, and of crimes against both the human and natural world. A nation dedicated to freedom while pursuing world empire and domination, a country promoting equality while initially condoning slavery and the destruction of native peoples, a land of opportunity which marginalizes ever-greater numbers of people – such a nation is, indeed, caught in a struggle with itself. But, as previously suggested, is this not the human condition: are we not each living between the promptings of our higher self, our spirit, and our shadow, revealing that which needs to be understood, integrated and transformed?

In describing the individual work of reconnection, I suggested that each of us is asked to find a new relationship to nature, to the earth and to our environment, to reconnect to the other and the human community and to find a more conscious relationship to the divine world and our individual spirit. This work is never done, and requires facing, acknowledging and seeking to transform our shadow by listening to the voice of conscience. Why should it be any different for American society, with the shining light of its spirit, its goodness, generosity of heart and practical wisdom and skill, and its arrogance and naked pursuit of wealth and power described in the essay on the pattern and ideology of oppression (Chapter 10).

We are individually and collectively in the same boat; how do we become more caring, loving human beings while creating a society which fosters equality, relationship, opportunity, freedom and love? In his marvelous work on the American Soul, Needleman notes this deep connection between the forms of society and our inner soul states:

The hope of America lies and has consisted in the fact that its political ideals and forms of government, its iconic actions and archetypal heroes, reflect in two directions at once – towards the external good of a life of liberty and equality and the reasonable search for a life of community and creative aspiration, and at the same time inwardly toward the search for inner development, the life of conscience and reason that defines the true nature of humanity and gives life its ultimate meaning.[2]

As there are moments of crisis in our life history – our evolving biography, which call us to reassessment, to ponder the meaning and purpose of our life, to face ourselves with clarity and conscience – so, too, are there crises in the evolving American story which challenge us to re-imagine what America is and can become. I believe we are again at such a point, in which the ideology of oppression and the forces of fear, hatred, egotism and division threaten to overwhelm us, and to neglect those founding principles and high ideals which marked the origin and development of this once-great nation.

Alexander Hamilton asked a profound question during the Constitutional Convention of 1787, regarding 'whether societies of men [and women] are really capable or not of establishing good government from reflection and choice, or whether they are forever destined to depend for their political constitutions on accident and force'.[3] He and many of the founding fathers saw the creation of the new nation as an experiment, as an effort to move history in the direction of reason, enlightenment and divine grace. The answer to Hamilton's question is still open. We are again at a time of great testing, as we were during the Revolutionary War, the Civil War and the Great Depression leading to the Second World War. It seems that about every 80 years, roughly four generations, we face a profound and existential crisis to American democracy, as Howe and Strauss have pointed out in their generational study of US history, *The Fourth Turning*.[4]

I A Pattern of Crisis and Opportunity

It is of course possible to find many turning points in American history, but I believe there are four periods during which the survival and further development of American society was, or is again, threatened. The first of these was during the Revolutionary War period and the founding of the new republic, from approximately 1770 to 1787, from the time when tensions over taxation and representation between the 13 colonies and Great Britain began to grow, through the Revolutionary War, to the end of the Constitutional Convention in Philadelphia.

The second major threat to the country's future was from the 1850s to the formal end of the Civil War in 1866. The challenge to national sovereignty which the secession of the eleven slave-holding states of the Confederacy posed to federal authority was extreme, as was the division over the question of slavery. Between 600,000 and 750,000 soldiers died during the Civil War, more than in all other US wars combined.[5] The rancor of the conflict between the North and the South continues to this day, and is reflected in attitudes, speech and politics.

A third point of crisis and transformation occurred from 1928 to 1945, starting with the onset of the Great Depression and ending with the defeat of the Axis powers in 1945. And I would say that the fourth period of crisis started in 2001 with '9/11', and is ongoing, as I have attempted to show in the collected essays in this book.

In each of the three previous periods there were multiple challenges to the nation's future: first, the quite likely defeat of the new continental army by the British under General Howe and the possible failure of the 13 colonies to form an effective national government after the Revolutionary war. Then, during the Civil War, the threat of the long-term division of the country into two over the question of slavery and its extension into newly acquired territories. And in the early twentieth century, the Great Depression and the rise of fascism, Nazism and authoritarianism, which threatened the future of both Western economic life and the viability of democratic governments.

Today, it is the combination of US imperial ambitions, the profound levels of income inequality, the oligarchy of corporate wealth and power and the distinct authoritarian tendencies of the Trump administration, which pose a significant threat to our future as a democratic society. I say this because as I have shown in previous chapters, we face a crisis of identity; what kind of a country we will be, a political crisis about the nature of democracy and the rule of law, and an economic crisis about the sustainability and equity of our economic system. The Trump administration is the symbol and reality of societal trends which go back decades, and both Democrats and Republicans – indeed, all of us – carry some responsibility for a slide into authoritarianism, for the politics of global domination, for the corruption of our institutions, and for the oligopoly of wealth and privilege which we now have.

If we look to the past, then we can see that in each previous crisis a new imagination of America emerged, carried by leaders with courage, morality and conscience, who enlarged and extended opportunity, freedom and equality, and who gave a new and positive response to Hamilton's question about the viability of the American experiment. During the Revolutionary Period it was Washington, Franklin, Jefferson,

Adams, Madison and the other founding fathers who gained independence from Great Britain, and founded a new nation based on human rights and the consent of the governed, who created a democratic republic at the Constitutional Convention in Philadelphia in 1787.

During the Civil War period, it was Abraham Lincoln who, with great humility and wisdom, guided the nation through a time of great struggle, and who freed the slaves by the Emancipation Proclamation of 1863. At Gettysburg, in commemoration of the great loss of life, he rededicated the country to the pursuit of freedom and equality...

> that we here highly resolve that these dead shall not have died in vain... that this nation, under God, shall have a new birth of freedom... and that a government of the people, by the people, and for the people, shall not perish from the earth.[6]

Following the Great Depression, Franklin Delano Roosevelt proclaimed the 'New Deal', arguing that the central question the country faced during the Depression was whether or not 'individual men and women will have to serve some system of Government or economics or whether a system of Government and economics existed to serve individual men and women'.[7] The country, and the world, faced great struggles to stave off mass unemployment and starvation. Personal incomes dropped by over 50 per cent in the US, one third of all banks failed, and in 1931 unemployment reached over 25 per cent. Roosevelt argued for massive government intervention, and created multiple government programs to regulate the banking system, provide employment through the Civilian Conservation Corps and the Federal Relief Administration, and fostered greater economic security for American citizens through the Fair Labor Standards Act and the Social Security Administration. In foreign policy he supported China, France, England and the Soviet Union in their opposition to the emerging Axis Powers through Lend Lease and other measures.

In order to mobilize democratic societies during Second World War, Roosevelt also articulated the Four Freedoms during his third inaugural address to Congress in January of 1941. Freedom of Speech, Freedom of Worship, Freedom from Want and Freedom from Fear were his calls to the world, including in his speech the rights to economic opportunity, fair employment, to social security and to adequate health care.

Following Japan's attack on Pearl Harbor in December of 1941, Roosevelt led the American people into the Second World War, and helped secure the victory over Nazi Germany, fascist Italy and imperial Japan. Just before his death in April 1945, he also inaugurated plans for a lasting world peace through the United Nations, and a more stable international economic system through the creation of the International Monetary Fund (IMF) and the World Bank.[8]

In each of these three major crises in American history, it took political and moral imagination to found and then to extend democracy, to deepen the rule of law and to expand the realm of economic opportunity. It took leaders deeply committed to the founding ideals of freedom, democracy, equality and economic justice; to galvanize the nation into positively responding to the outer and inner challenges of these turning points in our history. Can we again find leaders with the moral imagination, the conscience and the vision to guide the American republic to a new and more noble chapter in its history? Can we overcome the pattern and ideology of oppression, of global domination and of economic exploitation which have characterized so much of our actions and policies in recent decades, and regain the respect of the global community, providing a beacon of hope for humanity? Can we again become 'the fact, the symbol and the promise of a new beginning'?[9]

II Re-Imagining America: Toward a New Covenant

Yesterday evening as I write, on a cold November night with new snow glistening on the roads and lawns, my wife and I were reading a book by Parker Palmer to each other. These words struck me:

> Fierce with reality is how I feel when I'm able to say 'I am that to which I gave short shrift and to that which I attended. I am my descents into darkness and my rising again into the light, my betrayals and my fidelities, my failures and my successes. I am my ignorance and my insight, my doubts and my convictions, my fears and my hopes.[10]

As an older person, I can increasingly say 'yes' to this, and I ask – can we as Americans also say 'yes' to our history, to our failures and successes, to our shame and to our achievements? Can we learn from our past, and recognize that we are again individually and collectively at a turning point in our history in which the issues we face are whether we can create a society capable of extending inner and outer freedom, fully honoring the equality of all human beings, and creating an economy which protects the needs of the earth and serves the aspirations of human beings for a life of dignity, respect and material well-being? I do not, of course, have an answer to this question, but I give full assent to Eleanor Roosevelt's view: 'We make our own history... the course of history is directed by the choices we make and our choices grow out of the ideas, the beliefs, the values, the dreams of our people.'[11]

What we will do in the coming decades, what leaders we will support and what kind of a society we will create is an open question. I, like many people engaged in the struggle of our times, have hopes, beliefs and ideas. Many of these I have shared in the earlier essays in this book, but now wish to weave into a more future-oriented tapestry – an imagination of what may be possible as policy and action. They are offered as a beginning for dialogue with the hope that we can move in the direction of a more democratic, just and free society, that we can transform the pattern and ideology of oppression into a society that can again become a beacon for the world.

Given the complexity of issues, what I have noted and suggested is an outline, a direction for consideration, and a set of possibilities to debate. The task is, in many ways, foolhardy; to delineate a new imagination for our American future in one essay. And yet I feel I have an obligation to attempt such a task, as I have focused so extensively on the recent deficiencies and limitations of the American experiment.

Despite the roar of the media and the rhetoric of division, we share much. Some 85 per cent of Americans favor net neutrality; 78 per cent want to get rid of Citizens United which allows corporations to pour unlimited amounts of money into politics; 68 per cent support stricter gun control; and 97 per cent want universal background checks. Over 80 per cent of Americans also want to see a more progressive tax system, with higher taxes for corporations and the wealthy. The majority of Americans also want more government action on climate change, want improved access to medical care, and support a legal path to citizenship for illegal immigrants and 'Dreamers'. We wish to see more spending on education, increased funding for infrastructure projects and are most tired of the corruption of our democratic system, giving Congress the abysmal approval rating of 19 per cent.[12]

So what is now needed to respond to the popular will, to that with which our hearts resonate, for ourselves, our children, our communities and, indeed, for the world? I believe some answers can emerge from the central gestures and accomplishments of our history, of our collective biography. These include:

1 We are a nation of immigrants, of refugees, and descendants of slaves from Africa, having displaced and marginalized the native peoples of this land who had lived here for thousands of years. I arrived here as a German immigrant at age seven. My wife's grandparents came from Sweden and Italy, and her grandmother on her mother's side was a descendant of Scottish settlers. Follow your own history and you will find similar patterns, or those of the legacy of slavery.

The nineteenth and twentieth centuries were a time of mass immigration, people escaping the famines, political revolutions and lack of opportunity in European nations. The dream of America, of economic opportunity and freedom, lured millions of people from all parts of the world. Between 1820 and 1930 over 4.5 million Irish people arrived on these shores, and during the same period over 5 million Germans. In the early twentieth century alone,12 million people entered the USA legally through Ellis Island, including over 4 million Italians and 2 million people of Jewish descent from Eastern Europe.[13] In recent decades it has been immigrants from Mexico and Latin America and from Asia who have sought entry into this country in increasing numbers.

Of course, there was always opposition; hatred, bigotry and racism leading, for example, to the Chinese Exclusion Act of 1882, or the Know Nothing Party, which sought to block all new immigrants in the late nineteenth century. And yet people came, drawn by a dream and much false advertising. The dream – the land of golden opportunity, the melting pot of races and cultures, and of new-found democracy and freedom – was most dramatically expressed in the famous lines from the poem by Emma Lazarus about the Statue of Liberty in New York harbor: '... give me your tired, your poor, your huddled masses yearning to be free', which many of us learned in school.[14]

Despite difficulty and opposition, people came and continue to come, looking for a better future.

2 We are the second most culturally and racially diverse large nation in the world, after Brazil. This is largely due to the fact that over 6 million African slaves were shipped to Brazil in the seventeenth, eighteenth and nineteenth centuries, while about half a million slaves were brought to and sold in the USA.

Today, whites make up over 60 per cent of the population, Latinos almost 18 per cent, African Americans 13 per cent, mixed race 6 per cent, Asian Americans a little over 6 per cent, and Native Americans, including Hawaiians, around 1.6 per cent.[15] It is estimated that by

2045, we will become a majority non-white population, with the Latino and Asian part of the population growing most rapidly in the coming decades. This is seen as tragic by white supremacists, and as a cause for celebration by many others. In my own case, my grandchildren are now part white, from different nations, part African American and part native American – a source of pleasure for my wife and me, and a harbinger of a future society in which race, ethnicity and sexual orientation will play a much smaller role in our society than the principle of individuality, than who we are as people.

3 The United States is one of the oldest constitutionally established democratic republics in the world, having neither succumbed to monarchy nor to dictatorship since its formal beginnings in the election of 1789. Since that beginning, it has gradually extended democratic rights to African Americans in 1863, and to women in 1920. The battle for true democracy continues with the forces of elitism, racism and misogyny always ready to curtail or limit our rights to vote, or to have our voices heard and counted in this age of media manipulation and special interest election funding.

4 America has been a prime mover in creating a global economy which, despite many limitations, has helped to diminish poverty and increase longevity around the world. By creating an international economic order through the IMF, the World Bank and the General Agreement on Tariffs and Trade (GATT) after the Second World War, and its insistence on legal protections for capital and private property, the USA has created the conditions for the largely unhindered movement of goods, labor and capital around the globe. It has also provided an indispensable ingredient for world trade through providing a stable key currency – the US dollar – to facilitate the many forms of international trade and travel. Whatever I have said about the pattern and ideology of oppression and of economic exploitation, which has been advanced and protected through these institutions, does not diminish the real achievements which a world economy has brought, and can bring, to humanity. The trade and movements of people, know-how and capital between countries is a net gain, and can become not only a benefit but a blessing, if structured properly.

5 The United States has also been a primary architect of the institutions of world peace and co-operation after the Second World

War through the creation of the United Nations, pushing for the UN Charter of Human Rights in 1946 and, at times, supporting the establishment and maintenance of democratic societies around the world. To be sure, there have been many lapses, supporting dictatorships, overthrowing democratically elected governments, launching many regional wars and presently being the world's largest military arms supplier, which of course exasperates the many armed conflicts still occurring.

6 America has also been the home of the civil rights movement, the women's movement and the environmental movement, fostering the establishment of multiple non-profit organizations doing the public good, thereby creating one of the most powerful civil society sectors in the world, and fostering the creation of civil society organizations globally. This has been a blessing for humanity, for without these organizations to press governments and businesses to act more responsibly, the issues we face would be even more severe, and the corruption more widespread.

7 For good and ill, Americans and US companies have pioneered the electronic revolution and the world wide web, supporting a global humanity awareness, as well as contributing to the dangers of surveillance, mind control, mass manipulation and screen addictions.

The twentieth century is often called 'the American century', when our way of life, our policies and the aforementioned achievements shaped the culture and institutions of the world. The question we now face as a people is whether we have the moral insight and wisdom to help guide humanity in the direction of a freer, more democratic, peaceful and economically just world in the present century? Can we use the soft power of being the city on the hill, the beacon of new hope for people around the world in this new century for global well-being? I think this is possible, if we overcome the old and stagnant arguments of right and left, and draw on our history and our collective conscience to truly create a government 'of the people, by the people and for the people', as Lincoln hoped at Gettysburg.

Such a new covenant, a new agreement, is based on a reciprocal relationship between citizens and their society. The primary responsibility of individuals is to seek to meet their physical, social and spiritual needs through their own efforts in the context of their community, and its norms and laws The responsibility of government at this time of growing individual awareness is to create the best conditions for individuals and groups, for its citizens, to achieve 'life, liberty and the pursuit of happiness', by fostering a maximum of freedom, a deep experience of equality as citizens of a democracy, and a creative economy which serves the needs of people and the earth. If I listen with my heart and turn to common sense, as well as draw on the policies and practices of other countries, I arrive at the following kind of measures.

I How Can We Restore and Deepen Democracy?

Since we now have the best democracy money can buy, let us consider taking the following steps:

- Voting is a right of individuals, not of groups and institutions. Ban all political donations from groups, non-profit organizations and political action committees for local, state and national campaigns. Only individual campaign contributions of $1,000, or less, would be allowed for individual campaigns and to political parties. Since there are many elections, and we know that discrepancies of wealth skew election outcomes, restrict total giving to all campaigns and parties to $5,000 per individual, per annum.
- Provide a public campaign financing option for state and national elections.
- To limit the power of parties and of special interest groups, introduce *ranked choice voting* in all local, state and national elections. This would be true of both primary and final election as is now the case for state elections in California and Maine. Ranked choice voting allows the two highest vote getters in primaries to run against each other in the final election, irrespective of party affiliation.
- Provide for term limits for Congress of three four-year terms for the House, lengthening terms from two to four years for the House, and providing for two six-year terms for the Senate. Also, prohibit lobbying activities for five years for all nationally elected representatives and all cabinet-level governmental appointees after they leave office.
- Hold state and national elections on a Saturday, on a date that is well established beforehand, as weekday elections discriminate against manual workers and other employees bound to a strict work schedule – something which is done in many other countries. Also, prohibit restrictive voter registration requirements, and allow all previously

convicted individuals to vote after they have served their terms, as was recently done in Florida.

- Set up independent multi-stakeholder re-districting commissions, including representatives from all political parties to establish new congressional districts based on new census data.
- Get rid of the undemocratic US Electoral College, and consider limiting the number of senators from states with less than 5 million people to one, rather than the two now allowed for each state. This means that 22 of the 52 states would have two, and the rest one, with both Wyoming and Vermont, with about half a million people each, being among that number.
- Provide for minimum-wage laws at a city and state level, indexed to local and regional living costs, sufficient to cover a modest living for a worker with up to two dependents.

If you have the urge to stop reading at this point because of either the projected costs, or the suspicion that I am putting forth a typical leftist agenda, let me assure you that I believe there is a way of financing these and other government programs through an Automatic Payment Transaction Tax (APT), of 0.35 per cent, and that I will promote views on education and culture more in keeping with conservative values.

- Expand Social Security for retirees by increasing the retirement age to 68, and increasing the salary limit for payment of Social Security tax to $250,000.
- Provide a Medicare-for-all insurance policy. What I mean by this is a single-payer system which is embodied in different bills now before Congress.
- Because increased automation will lead to decreased formal employment opportunities, consider a universal basic income for all children and adults of $12,500 per year at 2018 prices. Evidence suggests that such a step would lead to less addiction and less criminality, higher educational achievement and greater health and well-being. It will also enhance democracy. See such an income as a basic right, not tied to salary or social position. It will lead to economic growth and creativity in the economy, since the basic issue for developed economies is not enough demand, not enough consumption to buy the goods and services on offer.
- Select tri-sectoral commissions at the city, county, state and federal levels, consisting of representatives from business, the public sector, and

civil society, including educational institutions, with the authority to review and to propose legislation serving the public good to legislative bodies.

- Ensure the continued existence of a free press through legal and political means, and examine how best to regulate Google, Facebook, Microsoft and others in relation to the invasion of privacy, hate speech and false fear-mongering.

- Develop a large-scale, federally funded infrastructure program for roads, air transport and internet access. If you arrive in New York from Western Europe, Japan or China, you feel you have arrived in a developing country with pot-holed roads, decaying bridges and substantial blight.

- Adopt a green energy program, a 'Green New Deal', with the aim of replacing all fossil fuels by 2040. Provide government subsidies to locate manufacturing of alternative energy in rural hubs, with a particular focus on the Mid-West and South-West.

I have omitted a number of issues from this list, as I believe they require a high degree of international co-operation. These issues include the environment, migration and refugees, the global development of poor regions and states, war and conflict, the international arms trade, and the development and impact of AI and the web on children and on humanity, including the issues of surveillance and mind control. In the case of these issues, national governments do not have the reach to bring about the global solutions required.

You may think these policy prescriptions for extending and deepening our democracy are unrealistic, given the present political impasse between Republicans and Democrats. Since both parties now serve special interest groups, corporations and large financial institutions, we need to consider other strategies for mobilizing public opinion in favor of restoring our democracy. One approach is to consider creating a national agenda for political reform and social health by seeking to unite all civil society networks – the environmental movement, the social-justice movement, the women's movement, the anti-gun movement, the labor movement and the LBGT movement, as well as teachers and other educational groups behind a common set of principles and policies to create an American Covenant of Democratic and Human Rights. The stakes are remarkably high, for it is not only an authoritarian president we face, who is threatening humanity with his administration's stance on the environment, but also a coterie of corporate and financial interests who have forgotten that a healthy, equitable and democratic society is the best guarantor of a healthy economy.

For such a strategy to work, the political left needs to recognize that its secular, non-spiritual and anti-religious orientation offends many people who might otherwise agree with many policies fostering democratic and human rights. The Christian right, in turn, limits its appeal to ordinary voters by abandoning the deep appeal of Christ's teachings of love in the new Testament, in favor of what appears as a racist, misogynistic and anti-abortion appeal to Old Testament values.

For a new democratic majority to emerge, voters on both ends of the political spectrum must also jettison the old policy prescriptions of more government or more private enterprise, and come to see that a healthy society has three domains of activity – the cultural and civil society sector; the public, governmental sector; and the economic, business sector. In the USA, we live in a society where the business sector dominates both government and culture, bending society to its often short-term private interests, and seeking to control both government and culture in its search for profits. In some other countries, such as Iran, it is a dominant religious culture which controls the other two spheres; and in former communist countries or in China today, it is the state which controls both culture and business life. The most creative societies now and in the future will be those societies which honor freedom in the cultural sphere, equality within government, and the mutuality, service and efficiency in economic life. It really is a question of how do we best balance these three sectors of society for the common good, as suggested in the recent book *Free, Equal and Mutual: Rebalancing Society for the Common Good.*[16]

As I see the true seeds of deep reform slumbering within our nation's history, I see the long and still incomplete march of African Americans for lasting and true equality from slavery to the present and the women's movement, as the moral seed-bed for a new covenant between the American people and its government, a covenant for a new democracy. As Martin Luther King said at the March on Washington for Freedom and Jobs in August 1963:

> I still have a dream deeply rooted in the American dream – one day this nation will rise up and live up to its creed, – We hold these truths to be self-evident; that all men [people] are created equal.[17]

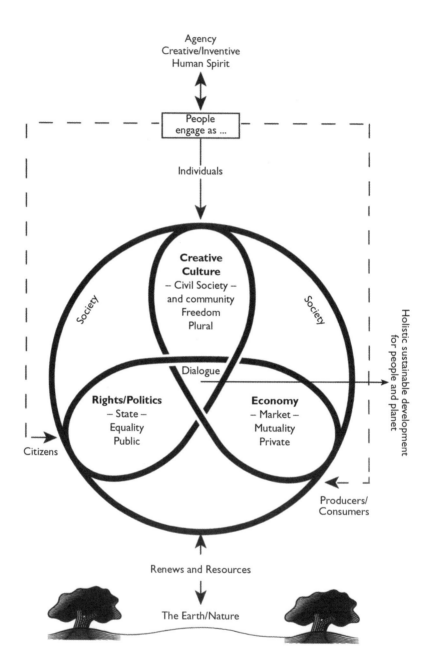

Agency
Creative/Inventive
Human Spirit

People
engage as ...

Individuals

**Creative
Culture**
– Civil Society –
and community
Freedom
Plural

Society

Society

Dialogue

Rights/Politics
– State –
Equality
Public

Economy
– Market –
Mutuality
Private

Citizens

Producers/
Consumers

Holistic sustainable development
for people and planet

Renews and Resources

The Earth/Nature

Figure 2 Rebalancing Society for the Common Good
(cf. Martin Large, *Free, Equal and Mutual*, 2018).

2 What Can We Do to Build a Just and Sustainable Stakeholder Economy?

How can we best achieve an economy which serves the needs of people, supports the communities in which businesses are located and which fosters environmental sustainability? I can see a number of interconnected approaches to move us in this direction.

- **Chartering Corporations**: The first step would involve adopting a version of the Accountable Capitalism Act recently proposed in the US Senate by Elizabeth Warren. It contains two main provisions: first, to charter all corporations with annual revenues exceeding $1 billion as US corporations, requiring those companies to honor the triple bottom line: profit, community and the environment. Such charters could be revoked if the company were not to honor the provisions of the charter and acted illegally. Secondly, the bill suggests that workers elect 40 per cent of Board members, as is done in Germany and some other Western European countries.[18]

  I would modify this bill in three ways, to lower the annual revenue figures from $1 billion to $500 million for national charters, to have the company charter renewed every ten years as part of an ongoing established evaluation process, and to broaden Board membership to include 30 per cent worker representation, but also 10 per cent representation from the governmental sector and 15 per cent from community and civil society organizations. This would mean that the power of shareholders and capital interests were sufficiently diluted so that they would need the support of other stakeholders to reach binding decisions. These boards would not only select management but also review company goals within the terms of the charter, and establish pay scales for management and labor.

  In addition to national corporate charters I would suggest state corporate charters for smaller and privately held corporations, with a review of charter compliance every five years. Again, the values of balancing profitability with social and community needs, and environmental sustainability, would need to be built into the charter and the compliance process.

The United States already has a rich history of seeking a responsible form of capitalism. The co-operative movement employs over two million people, and consists of 29,000 separate institutions which are all controlled by their members, with each member having one vote, regardless of their position or number of shares. There are also many employee-owned corporations, as well as companies which offer an Employee Stock Ownership Plan (or ESOP), as a way of promoting loyalty and improving retirement benefits. The B Corp and Benefit Corporation movement nationally and internationally honors the values of accountability, transparency of governance and decision-making, and clarity of purpose to provide a public benefit. Such corporations are a form of conscious capitalism seeking to balance the values of profitability, community benefit and environmental sustainability. This sector of business is growing rapidly and has in recent years garnered substantial capital investments.

Then there is the socially responsible investing movement which is moving large amounts of capital and pension money away from tobacco, arms, and polluting industries, and developing important yardsticks for measuring social responsibility and environmental sustainability. So, taken together with the public opposition to Citizens United, the worry about environmental sustainability, the legitimate concerns of the organized labor movement about the future of work, there is a public base for requiring corporations to be chartered and held to account through a regularly established and transparent charter review process at the state and federal level. This step, when taken together with limiting the ability of corporations and the wealthy to skew political outcomes through large hidden political donations, would go a long way toward restoring democracy and healing an economy which now serves the wealthy and the powerful, and is clearly destroying the earth.

- **Supporting Natural Capitalism**: Globally, the economy uses a flow of half a trillion tons of materials a year, but only 1 per cent is then embodied in products: the rest is wasted. By *increasing resource productivity* through the re-design of production processes, the first of four principles of natural capitalism; costs decrease and environmental sustainability is enhanced. *Eliminating the concept of waste* is the second principle. Thus, when the BMW corporation is able to recycle over 90 per cent of demo models and other used vehicles, or a Swiss furniture manufacturer designs office chairs using natural materials, and recycles its water so that it emerges cleaner than the city water it initially used, both companies are valuing their environmental inputs. The environmental services which nature provides are often seen as free, and pollution is seen as an externality that can be charged to the general public. Yet environmental services, which

156

'include nutrients and water, regulating atmosphere and climate, providing pollination and biodiversity, controlling pests and diseases and assimilating and detoxifying society's waste, are extremely valuable.... Indeed their value is nearly infinite for without them there is no life and therefore no economic activity. But none of their value is reflected in anyone's balance sheet.'[19]

The third principle of natural capitalism is *moving toward a solutions economy*, meaning shifting from the selling of products to providing services, such as Carrier does when it provides 'comfort services', including heating, cooling and air quality, by providing machines, services and maintenance through an annual contract to consumers.

The fourth principle of natural capitalism is *re-investing in natural capital*, through large-scale re-cycling, environmental remediation, and air and water purification.

Using these four principles, which have been applied by large and small companies around the world for several decades, economic activity would begin to learn from and mimic the profound wisdom of nature in its eco-system interdependency and co-operation, its web of life. Natural life systems, the relation between plants, insects, birds and other animals, show a remarkable mutually transformative, context sensitive, reciprocal life-enhancing sensitivity, which we ignore at our peril if we wish to survive.

Natural capitalism is based on the revolutionary book by Paul Hawkens, Amory Lovins and L.Hunter Lovins, *Natural Capitalism: Creating the Next Industrial Revolution*, and the research and consultancy work of the Rocky Mountain Institute.[20] The direction and methods of this institute, and of the many initiatives which support local sustainable economic networks, would be enormously enhanced by taxing natural inputs and pollution. Thus, a *Carbon Tax*, a *Land Tax* and a *Water Pollution Tax* would serve to push innovative businesses in the direction of using natural materials much more efficiently and sustainably.

I have discussed the challenges of modern capitalism in three previous essays, 'The Crisis of Western Capitalism' (Chapter 4), 'Reflections on the Global Economic Crisis and What to Do About It' (Chapter 5) and 'Toxic Excess: Income Inequalities and the Fundamental Social Law' (Chapter 7). What was not so clearly stated in those essays is that capitalism rests on three questionable assertions – namely, that nature, labor and capital are commodities to be bought and sold by the market to the highest bidder regardless of the consequences. The natural environment belongs to the commons, and taxing its use and misuse is clearly in the best interests of humanity.

- **Supporting a Guaranteed Basic Income**: Wages have been largely stagnant in the United States since the late 1970s, when adjusted for inflation, due in part to companies rewarding investors and top management more than the ordinary worker. With the growth of international trade and globalization, larger companies have also moved production to low-wage countries, and the manufacturing base of the country has been eroded. These developments, when coupled with automation and the financial crisis of 2008–10, have led to the greatest income inequalities the country has seen since just before the Great Depression. The many negative effects of such disparities of income and wealth were captured in the slogan of 'The 1 per cent and the 99 per cent', brought to public awareness by the Occupy Movement, and described in some detail in the earlier essay, 'Toxic Excess: Income Inequalities and the Fundamental Social Law' (Chapter 7).

Since 70 per cent of the US economy is based on domestic consumption, and over 50 per cent of Americans are struggling to just get by, a Guaranteed Basic Income would go a long way to restoring long-term economic growth and would also strengthen democracy, whilst also working to mitigate the physical and psychological effects of poverty. It would also allow caretakers and stay-at-home parents to receive a stipend for their important work of raising children, and of taking care of the sick and elderly.

I have proposed a Guaranteed Basic Income of $12,500 per person per annum at 2018 prices. This direct payment would go to every child and adult, regardless of financial circumstances. It would replace all other Federal Welfare Programs, but not affect Social Security.

A Guaranteed Basic Income is presently being experimented with in India, Finland and Canada. A four-year trial was also undertaken in Dauphin, Manitoba in the mid-1970s, with the result that school graduation rates rose, hospital visits decreased, crime was reduced, and life satisfaction increased.[21] Also, full- and part-time employment was not affected in significant ways, undercutting the argument that such an income would undermine the labor market and lead to a decline in employment. Common sense would suggest that, instead, it would lead to improved wages at the lower end of the pay scale.

It would also be a practical step to limiting wage slavery, the necessity of working to just stay alive and selling one's labor to the highest bidder, rather than working to contribute in a meaningful way to society. I believe it would also enhance democracy and lead to a flourishing of cultural life. Harper Lee, for example, managed to write *To Kill a Mockingbird*, because she was given a year's stipend to just write, whereas before this she only managed to publish a few short stories, as she previously had to find part-time employment just to survive.

Opposition to the idea of a Guaranteed Income is mainly focused on the large costs associated with such a program and its likely effect on migration rates, with the German government recently opposing such a measure because of the fear of increased immigration. I think that an Automatic Payment Transaction Tax of 0.35 per cent would fund such a program, and be sufficient to support the other policy measures I have suggested.

- **Adopting an Automatic Payment Transaction Tax (APT)**: The Gross National Product (GDP) of the United States was a little over $19 trillion in 2017. Of that total, about $6.9 trillion was levied in federal, state and local taxes, including both corporate and local property taxes. American citizens paid an average of about 30 per cent of their income in taxes that year. All national, state and local governmental activities and services, as well as public education, were funded from these tax receipts. Whilst GDP was over $19 trillion in 2017, which was the value of the actual goods and services purchased and sold in the USA, including international trade, the financial transactions which circulated in the financial or monetary economy were much greater than that – perhaps in excess of $1,000 trillion a year.[22] This figure includes new money being deposited in bank accounts, deposits into non-bank accounts, trades on the New York Stock Exchange and Nasdaq, the purchase and sale of Treasury bills, the trade in bonds and derivatives, as well as all international capital transfers.

  So if we adopted an Automatic Payment Transaction Tax (APT) on all financial transactions – from purchasing a movie ticket, to purchasing a car, to buying a house or stock in a company – we would be not only taxing the money moving through the real economy – $19 trillion – but also the vast amounts of money circulating through the speculative money economy – $1,000 trillion or more a year. Such a tax of just

0.35 per cent, on both money spent and received, was first proposed in 2005 by the economist Edgar Feige to Bush's Panel on Tax Reform, was reviewed positively by the *New York Times*, and is, I believe, the fairest and politically most feasible approach to replacing our expensive, often corrupt and inadequate tax system.

An Automatic Payment Transaction Tax of 0.35 per cent was judged to be revenue-neutral in 2005, and would probably yield even larger amounts of tax revenue today. Such a tax could also be adjusted and increased to fund a Single Payer Health System, the Green New Deal and a Guaranteed Basic Income.[23] It is also easy to implement, given the automated nature of our financial system, and it is difficult to scam. It would also, over a process of gradual implementation, replace all income taxes, sales taxes and corporate taxes, and lower local property taxes by covering the educational component of such taxes which constitute over 60 per cent of most town and city taxes. It would also limit the volatility of financial markets, and be progressive in the sense that it would affect those trading and speculating in the stock and financial markets more than ordinary citizens. What is not to like about this fair approach to taxing money when it enters and moves through both the financial system and real economy?

I find it intriguing that despite the technical ability to collect such a tax, and the difficulty of gaming the system, given the electronic trail left by such transactions, it has not surfaced as a significant topic of public debate and an obvious answer to the dilemmas of the deficit and the government funding of programs. I am sure this is because of the enormous hidden political power of the financial industry, both nationally and internationally. What would happen if the 99 per cent took up this banner, and one or both political parties made it part of their national platform?

- **Creating Producer–Consumer–Trade–Financing Networks**: One of the lessons of Community Supported Agriculture (CSA) and fair trade networks is the positive effect such networks can have on the lives of producers and consumers by establishing direct connections between farmers and their customers in the regional economy. Could this not be done on a broader basis, so that at a county and regional level, a conscious dialogue would take place between a variety of producers, consumers, retail and financing organizations seeking to meet the needs of local communities in an area? An assessment of gaps in products and services, the difficulty of marketing and distribution or of finding adequate warehousing and affordable retail spaces, or the need for long-term financing, could be ascertained by these consultative bodies. Such groups would perceive needs and gather information for shaping economic life to everyone's benefit. Such a step would mimic the communication and mutual support which nature provides. As Peter Wohleben remarks in the *Hidden Life of Trees*,

> But why are trees such social beings? Why do they share food with others of their own species and sometimes even go so far as nourish their competitors? The reasons are the same as for human communities: there are advantages to working together.[24]

I earlier mentioned that capitalism treats land and the environment, labor and capital as commodities, and does not take into account that land, water and air are also part of the commons upon which we all depend, that labor is what we offer to our community, and that capital represents our collective savings. By chartering corporations, supporting natural capitalism, providing a basic guaranteed income and adopting an APT tax, we redress the balance of power which corporations have over our lives, and we foster the common good. We are then also supporting a life of dignity for all human beings, and unleashing the creativity of individuals in society.

3 How Can We Protect and Extend Freedom in Cultural Life?

Built into our constitution is the right to free speech, of a free press, the right of assembly and the free exercise of religion. Since our founding, American society has attempted to realize these rights. But now they are under a sustained assault. The illegal mass surveillance of the population by the NSA (National Security Administration), the FBI, the CIA and other governmental agencies was revealed by the leak of government documents by Edward Snowden. Such gathering of information was made possible by the passage of the Patriot Act, following the terror attacks of 9/11, the later Homeland Security Act and the renewal of the main provisions of the US Patriot Act through the US Freedom Act in 2015. If we add to this threat the selling of personal information to third parties by Google and Facebook, and the manipulation of news sent to private e-mails by groups such as Cambridge Analytica and Russian trolls, we seem to be in unchartered territory in which our every movement in known, and our minds and thoughts manipulated by the ever-present power of the internet.

The awesome power which governments and corporations now have over what we do, what we think and what we experience as truth and consider reality, is truly frightening. As one observer remarked, '…today we live in a society in which spurious realities are manufactured by the media, by governments, by big corporations, by religious groups, political groups…. I do not distrust their motives; I distrust their power.'[25] If we add to this that our president dominates the global news cycle, attacks the free press and manufactures lies without end, then we have to accept that we live in dystopian times in which the very basis of democracy is undermined. For democracy depends upon dialogue and consensus, and this in turn is dependent on an agreement about discernable facts. But when truth becomes no more than personal opinion, common ground cannot be found, and society risks being torn apart.

I have suggested different ways in which we can take personal responsibility for what we see and believe in the essay on 'Looking for Hope in Difficult Times' (Chapter 9), and would add that we can individually and collectively deepen our power of discernment and a sense for truth in working on our own development, as described in 'Facing Ourselves: The Work of Reconnection' (Chapter 11). We can also seek legal remedies for controlling Google, Facebook and other internet news providers, seeking to balance freedom of speech and the public interest – as many European nations have recently done, and as is presently being considered, as I write, by the US Congress. To stop mass surveillance of US citizens will be difficult, but the US Freedom Security Act is up for renewal in 2019, and the ACLU (American Civil Liberties Union) is actively seeking remedies for the unwarranted and intrusive invasion of privacy rights by the Government. We can also take courage from Hannah Arendt's insight that demagogues share a fatal flaw: 'the deceivers started with self-deception', and ultimately Trump will be caught in a collapsing bunker of his own making.[26] I believe this is finally happening, as neither allies nor supporters can continue to wink and laugh at the daily chaos he is creating. My supposition is that the president will have resigned before the election of 2020 in order to protect his family's interests and assets, while blaming the Democrats and 'fake news' for driving him out of office.

We have rightly valued the freedoms embodied in the US Constitution and the first Amendment. We must protect them vigorously, and must seek to extend them into the realm of education, for nothing is more important in the long run to the future of democracy and a healthy society than an excellent and diverse education system.

Since the country's founding, primary, secondary and higher education in the United States has been a mixture of public and private institutions. Ten per cent of children in PK-12 attend private schools – including Catholic and religious schools, Montessori academies, Waldorf schools and college prep schools. Over half of the colleges and universities in the United States are private non-profit institutions, including many of our elite universities, such as Harvard, Yale and Stanford. While this diversity of educational choice is admirable, access to private schools and universities is limited to the wealthiest segment of the population.

If I am right about the revenue resulting from an Automatic Payment Transaction Tax (APT), then our society would be able to provide all educational institutions with a regionally based tuition grant per student from PK through high school and for colleges and universities, sufficient to improve teacher–student ratios and enhanced educational excellence. Taking such a step would result in competition between different educational institutions for students and parental support. As schools have different philosophies of education and different views of child development, such grants would create a level playing-field between them, and parents would have a choice for their children in expressing their values, religious beliefs and educational goals, as would students attending colleges and graduate school.

There are a variety of arguments which favor such a step. We already recognize freedom of speech and religion. Parents care deeply about their children, and the values and beliefs to which they are exposed in school. By creating a level playing-field between different types of educa-tional systems and their competing philosophies, we would be extending freedom of educational choice to the majority of the population, which presently do not have such a choice because they cannot afford private education. Also, we would be recognizing that public education is not value neutral: it has a view of child development and the purposes of education, even though they are seldom clearly articulated.

If you were to compare the values of a military academy, an arts-oriented junior high school, a Quaker Academy, a Waldorf school, a Christian school and a public school, and were to have conversations about the aims of education and the details of the curriculum, you would have a great diversity of opinions. As, in my experience, both children and parents know when the education is working for them, and children have different, unique learning styles and needs, why not extend educational options and choices to all? If resource allocation is roughly comparable, as they are to some degree in a few European countries and in Australia, you would have an increase in educational innovation and creativity. Diversity of educational approaches, like diversity of people and of art, is to be celebrated and supported, and uniformity and regimentation of education and culture are to be avoided, as they are the hallmarks of authoritarian societies.

The main argument against taking such a step is the threat of racial or religious discrimination. Could this danger not be dealt with by laws barring such discrimination?

It seems to me that there are two main threats to educational freedom today: the pressure from the State to impose value and curriculum priorities on schools, as was done to some degree by the No Child Left Behind Act and the Obama administration's Every Student Succeeds Act; and secondly, the pressure from corporations to achieve efficiency through privatization and the adoption of machine learning technologies and methods. The sensitivity of parents to both of these intrusions has come to express itself in the Opt-Out Movement and in the growth of Home Schooling in recent years. In 2013, a little under two million children were involved in the home-schooling movement, and the numbers have increased since then. So why not expand educational opportunity and choice? To do so would also encourage the parent, family, school and community partnerships which educational researchers recognize as a vital factor in educational achievement. If each school has its own governing board of parents, teachers and community members, as well as parent–teacher associations, as many private schools now have, would this not encourage a focus on the learning needs of children?

The arguments against diversity and competition in education, in particular against charter schools, have focused on the perceived threat to public education resulting from the loss of funds. If you have more resources available to education in general through an Automatic Payment Transaction Tax (APT), this threat is removed. Yes, there is still the challenge in poorer neighborhoods and rural regions of too-limited knowledge and parental support for education, but a Guaranteed Basic Income and equitable funding formulae between richer and poorer regions would, over time, level the playing field and could lead to lower class sizes and improved teacher salaries.

Governmental institutions with elected representatives have the tendency to work toward equality and uniformity of services, as they should. Yet this also means that the State has the tendency to work toward standardization in educational programs and outcomes, and to impose its view of the purposes and nature of the education. This tendency works against diversity of educational values and activities. The State should only be involved in assuring equality of access to educational options, providing for conditions of safety and assuring adequate educational outcomes at the junior high school, and high-school graduation level. State and county educational authorities could determine funding formulae, safety conditions and minimum achievement levels required for graduation, and leave parents, teachers and community representatives to guide individual schools and region-wide school options. The National Association of Independent Schools (NAIS) already has a well-developed process for accrediting diverse schools. Let it become a broader association of all primary and secondary schools, and carry out its work of assuring educational quality against the aims, values and programs of each school's charter with periodic evaluations. The same can be done for colleges and universities.

The threat to education and the teacher–student relationship from machine learning will only grow in the coming years, as the argument is made that a machine learning program will allow for all learning to be tailored to the student's individual progress, and at a much lower cost. Why have teachers at all, when all knowledge can be web accessed and all lesson plans made available? We can be sure that the pressure to move in this direction will continue to grow from private corporations and internet giants such as Microsoft, Apple, Amazon, Google and Facebook. The only sure defense against the resulting student isolation from others, the loss of the learning community, and the undermining of the human relation between student and teacher is to allow parents, children and teachers to have educational choices – witness the popularity of Montessori and Waldorf schools in Silicon Valley, and the limitation which those parents place on their children's use of net devices.

In addition to fostering educational diversity and choice, increased resources for the arts could be made available through the regional and state-wide arts councils that now exist. The arts are undervalued in our secular technological culture, despite their vital role in fostering creativity and nourishing the human soul. Many European societies recognize this, and provide much more support for the arts than is done here. Let us reverse this trend, and recognize that a flourishing arts scene is an essential part of a vibrant and healthy culture and society.

4 Fostering a Tri-Sectoral Society and Honoring the Principle of Individuality

By deepening and extending democracy through honoring our equality as human beings, promoting a stakeholder economy and protecting and deepening our experience of freedom in education and culture, we would create societal conditions which would allow the individuality of each human being to thrive. We would be creating the outer conditions which encourage each person to develop their uniqueness through encouraging their educational, cultural, philosophical and religious preferences, to experience their equality as citizens of a democratic society, and to contribute to an economy that serves people and the earth.

I believe such a society would help us to balance our natural egotism and go a long way toward answering the central concerns of both left and right. It would respond to the concerns of the political right about the encroachment of the State into the religious, spiritual and cultural preferences of the individual and the family, and the concerns of the left about inequality and economic justice. Critical to moving in this direction is limiting the power of corporations to manipulate politics through political donations, and by chartering all corporations; by providing citizens with a Guaranteed Basic Income, and by promoting educational alternatives and funding a diverse network of educational initiatives and institutions. Funding for such steps, and a universal healthcare system, could be achieved through adopting a national and international APT tax, as previously described.

What would help such a restructuring of society and stimulate a conscious awareness in people that we naturally seek freedom in cultural life, equality in the realm of government and politics, and mutuality and shared benefit in economic life, would be *citizen councils* which honor these different aspects of our nature. Citizen councils consisting of representatives from culture and civil society, government and business life could be created to assist legislative bodies by reviewing and proposing policies as previously suggested. Representatives from these same sectors would sit on corporate boards to see that corporations honor the conditions of their charter and the triple bottom line. And producer, consumer, finance and trader networks could be encouraged in order to perceive economic needs, and establish economic priorities for a region.

The same principle of honoring stakeholder interests could also be applied in the realm of education, where school and college boards and regional educational authorities would consist of teachers, parents, administrators and people from business and politics. In this way we would create a tri-sectoral stakeholder society that seeks to honor the interests of each sector, while also helping individuals to exercise their freedom, equality and mutuality. By honoring 'these truths', we would renew and extend the American Dream, and move toward an empowered, creative society.

5 International Issues: Does America Have a Global Responsibility?

I mentioned earlier that there is a range of issues requiring international co-operation and action. These include climate change, migration and refugees, regional economic development in the poorer regions of the earth; war, including nuclear weapons and regional conflicts, terrorism, and the intrusions of machines, robots and artificial intelligence (AI) and mass surveillance into our lives. In seeking to meet these international threats to human well-being, the United States faces the basic question of whether it will retreat into an 'America first', nationalist stance, or whether we will again become a world leader in supporting humanity's collaborative effort to meet these mounting challenges. Our history in creating the United Nations, being a multi-racial, multi ethnic, democratic society, helping to create a world economy and championing the cause of human rights provides a basis for again recognizing and acting to promote freedom, democracy, and economic prosperity globally. Can we transform the push for World Empire, for military hegemony, and for economic dominance, to again become a leader of true human aspirations?

If we make progress in overcoming the pattern and ideology of oppression (discussed at length earlier) in our own society, then we will have a moral basis for promoting meaningful and much-needed change on the world stage. Out of new insight and a new commitment to the political and social truths underlying the American experiment, by creating a new Threefold Covenant of Cultural, Democratic and Economic Rights, as previously outlined, we will be moved as a people and a society to join the many international efforts to improve the human condition. This means wholeheartedly supporting the United Nations and its many programs of international assistance, including the recent UN-sponsored Global Compact for Migration, signed by 165 governments in Morocco in December 2018, but opposed by the United States.[27]

There are presently over 250 million people living outside the countries of their birth, and over 60 million refugees, some living in camps for generations. By signing the Global Compact and developing a transparent and fair immigration policy ourselves, including a path to citizenship for illegal immigrants and honoring the citizenship rights of children born in this country to immigrants ('Dreamers'), we would join the global community in seeking answers to the growing movement of people across borders and regions. We should also take a leadership role in the United Nations in promoting a massive global effort to promote societal health in the poorer regions of the earth, thereby limiting the need to flee violence, hunger and a lack of opportunity. Promoting freedom in cultural life, and a vibrant civil society movement, democracy and equality in politics, and a healthy and sustainable economy, a tri-sectoral imagination of societal health, such an effort could become a blessing for humanity. A sizeable portion of a global Automatic Payment Transaction Tax could devote trillions of dollars to such an effort, and be linked to limiting global warming and providing for renewable energy growth in the poorer regions of the earth. We could also devote a portion of our huge defense budget to helping other societies achieve a higher degree of social health. If we moved in this direction, we would be honoring our past, our history and the ideals which have made the United States a beacon of hope for so many people around the globe, and we would be infinitely safer.

If we are concerned about climate change, as the majority of US citizens are, then we must also rejoin the Paris Climate Accords, from which the current Trump administration has withdrawn, and seek to heed the warnings of both the major Climate Report from the UN, and the more recent National Climate Assessment compiled by multiple US governmental agencies. Unless more action is taken now, we will realize a temperature rise of 2.7 degrees by 2040, according to the UN, and this will lead to vastly increased flooding, famines, drought, poverty and violence, as people struggle to survive. Given the interconnection of global issues, such an increase in temperature would also lead to catastrophic waves of forced migration, flooding host countries with unwanted refugees. The US governmental report echoes these warnings, and both reports suggest that to prevent these developments, greenhouse gases must be reduced by 30 per cent globally by 2030, and renewable energy sources increased from 20 per cent today to 67 per cent by 2040.[28] As the world's largest economy and the pace-setter in so many areas of public life, let us become a leader in environmental sustainability, in alternative energy, and in international efforts to preserve humanity's future.

We need to add the recognition of the global humanity threat of Artificial Intelligence (AI) to the threat of environmental collapse. If I had not forgotten the warnings of Joseph Weizenbaum, which the MIT computer scientist already conveyed to me in the early 1970s and been more alert to these dangers earlier, I would have included a section on this threat in the earlier essay on the 'The Ideology of Oppression' (Chapter 10). As it is, I believe this is as great a threat to our human future as the destruction of the natural environment, and I strongly advise readers to delve into these questions.[29]

If we adopt an international approach to the environment, to the challenges of international migration and to the grave dangers of Artificial Intelligence, then other vexing issues such as the international arms race, nuclear weapons and terrorism, as well as the dangers of global poverty and strife, can be worked on and given the resources they require. There is a great deal of both governmental and non-governmental expertise available in each of these areas that can be mobilized, if the political will can be found to serve humanity's global needs.

It is not lack of knowledge which stops us making progress on the most pressing issues facing humanity, but lack of political leadership, of a common will, and, in many cases, inadequate funding. Given the large amount of agreement among both American citizens and a global population about the issues of greatest concern, let us activate ourselves and help the United States again take a leadership role in promoting human decency, common sense and a stakeholder society. As part of this effort, and in recognition of the vital role civil society can play in exposing the power alliances of big business and big government, let us also promote a *World Parliament* of civil society representatives, as a sister organization to the United Nations, in order apply pressure on national governments and international groups for meaningful global change.

6 Toward a Strategy of Hope

I have suggested that American Society is again at a time of great challenge in which the future of our democracy and our role in the world are at stake, as they have been about every 80 years during our history. I believe we have ended up in this situation because political and economic elites have manipulated the American public into supporting a Global Empire Project following 9/11, have distorted the economic system to serve the powerful and the wealthy, and in the process they have severely compromised democracy through hidden money and corruption. Because the gap between who we say we are as a society and a nation, and how we have actually behaved, has increased dramatically since at least the beginning of the twenty-first century, a soul space of disappointment and disillusionment was created in the national psyche which Trump and the forces of our collective American shadow have exploited to lead us astray.

A *strategy of hope* begins by seeing ourselves clearly, by self-knowledge, by being awake, and by recognizing the ways in which we as a nation have served the gods of power, prejudice, aggression, pride and material wealth, while proclaiming the values of human freedom, decency, peace, equality and economic opportunity. It means recognizing that we all live within what Parker Palmer calls the 'tragic gap' as individuals and a nation:

> On the one side of the gap, we see the hard realities of the world, realities which can crush our spirits and defeat our hopes. On the other side of that gap, we see real-world possibilities, life as we know it could be because we have seen it that way.[30]

When the experience of this gap is sufficiently painful, we create communities of conscience, groups of the heart, which have always moved our society in a positive direction in the past, and will continue to do so in the future. The young people at Marjorie Douglas High School in Parkland, Florida, who recently founded the #Never Again Movement, did just that in fighting for gun control. As David Hogg noted,

> When it happened to us, we woke up. We knew we couldn't wait until we got out of college and settled into jobs. We had to make the world a better place now. It was literally a matter of life and death.[31]

So let us honor, join and support the many groups promoting environmental sustainability, freedom of speech and worship, educational choice, racial justice, labor rights, women's equality, democratic reform, peace and economic justice – groups which make up the vast network of civil society nationally and globally. While we can only see the future in our imagination, out of our experience of life we do know our yearning for greater inner and outer freedom, our desire for greater equality in rights and political life, and our wish for right livelihood and economic justice. Could we therefore not agree as individuals and groups to re-imagine an America which:

1 **Honors the multicultural and multi-racial nature of our society, welcoming refugees and immigrants;**

2   Supports our international and global role in promoting peace, freedom, equality and economic justice as well as environmental sustainability, through a UN-sponsored set of economic, social and educational development plans for the world;

3   Promotes an excellent and diverse educational and cultural life by supporting a greater variety of educational options and a flowering of cultural expression through improved funding and free access to education and the arts;

4   Supports democratic reform by removing institutional and dark money from the political process, and improving voter rights and access;

5   Recognizes the importance of a healthy, sustainable economy by chartering corporations and fostering natural capitalism;

6   Creates greater economic equity and overcomes the toxic effect of wealth inequalities by providing a Guaranteed Basic Income of $12,500 a year per person, beginning in childhood; and

7   Provides the resources for this and other programs such as Universal Healthcare, by adopting a national and international Automatic Payment Transaction tax (APT).

Could such an effort at a free, equal and mutual society, of a tri-sectoral imagination of our social future, form a new Covenant between the American people and its government, appealing to both conservatives and progressives? Would it also not honor the deeper gestures and achievements of our history, giving new hope to people of all persuasions wishing to see a brighter future? Promoting such a covenant – 'going public', as Parker Palmer calls this step in the process of social reform – involves creating cross-sectoral networks of influence, networks which bridge specific issue-oriented groups, and which cross party and ideological lines.[32]

I believe this can be done, if we have patience and moral courage. Then signs of success begin to appear, as I think they already are doing, for a Guaranteed Basic Income, Universal Medical Care and Diversity and Free Access to Education. But not without struggle and sacrifice, and a new, moral and dedicated democratic leadership, which can help us to meet this fourth great set of challenges in our history.

So let us seek help from the good spirit of America, say 'yes' to a new future, and follow Rebecca Solnit's advice:

Dream big. Occupy your hopes.
Talk to strangers. Live in public.
Don't stop now.[33]

Notes

1   Jill Lepore, *These Truths: A History of the United States*, W.W. Norton, New York, 2018, p. 786.

2   Jacob Needleman, *The American Soul: Rediscovering the Wisdom of the Founders*, Tarcher/Putnam, New York, 2002, p. 19.

3   Lepore, *These Truths*, p. xvii.

4   See the fascinating study by William Strauss and Neil Howe, *The Fourth Turning: An American Prophecy*, Bantam/Doubleday, New York, 1997. Strauss and Howe call the period in which we now find ourselves the Millennial Crisis, lasting from 2005 to 2026, having also identified the Revolutionary Period, the Civil War and the New Deal Era as periods of crisis and transition in our history. See pp. 123–138.

5   Avery Craven, Walter Johnson and Roger Dunn, *A Documentary History of the American People*, Ginn and Company, New York, 1951. See the commentaries on the US Constitution from the Federalist papers, pp. 186–194, and the Constitution with the articles of amendment, pp. 194–205.

6   Craven, Johnson, Dunn, *A Documentary History*, p. 409.

7   Ibid., p. 718.

8   Lepore, *These Truths*, pp. 433–471.

9   Needleman, *The American Soul*, p. 5.

10   Parker Palmer, *On the Brink of Everything: Grace, Gravity and Getting Old*, Berret-Koehler, San Francisco, Calif., 2018, pp. 15, 16.

11   Quoted by Jon Meacham, *Time Magazine*, 12 November 2018.

12   See www.Care 2, Kevin Mathews, 22 February 2018.

13   See US Immigration, www.history.com. Also Lepore, pp. 311–360.

14   Emma Lazarus, 'The New Colossus', www.poetryfoundation.org.

15   William Frey, 'U.S. Population', 14 March 2018; www.brookings.edu.

16   See the socially perceptive and innovate study by Martin Large and Steve Briault (eds), *Free, Equal and Mutual: Rebalancing Society for the Common Good*, Hawthorn Press, Stroud, UK, 2018, in particular M. Large, 'Rebalancing society for the common good', pp. 99–116. The diagram is borrowed from this chapter, p. 115.

17   Martin Luther King, 'I Have a Dream' Speech, Washington, D.C, 28 August 1963. See www.archives.gov/press/exhibits/dream speech pdf.

18   The Accountable Capitalism Act; www.warren.senate.gov.

19   www.natcapsolutions.org, 'Natural Capitalism: Path to Sustainability?'.

20   Paul Hawkins, Amory Lovins, L. Hunter Lovins, *Natural Capitalism: Creating the Next Industrial Revolution*, Rocky Mountain Institute, Snowmass, Colo., 2018. An updated edition of a book first published in 1998.

21   Ashifa Kasan, 'Ontario Pilot Project puts Universal Basic Income to test', *Guardian* newspaper, 28 October 2016.

22   It is hard to get a real figure on the amount of money circulating in the financial economy. Scott Smith, in *The New Operating System for the American Economy*, pp. 23–25; www.TheFoundationForaBetterEconomy.org, 2017, pp. 23–25, argues that it is as much as 5,000 trillion, but I think this is an exaggeration. His book is interesting in its boldness, but it also gives the false impression that Mr Smith invented the idea of a Financial Transaction Tax, which is far from the truth, given its past history as an idea discussed in economics and passed into legislation by numerous governments.

23   See the website www.apttax.com/ for a detailed discussion of the Automatic Payment Transaction Tax, including objections, questions and concerns as well as access to the more academic articles of Dr Feige.

24   Peter Wohlleben, *The Hidden Life of Trees: The Illustrated Edition*, Greystone Press, Vancouver, 2018, pp. 8, 12.

25   Brooke Gladstone, *The Trouble with Reality: A Rumination on Moral Panic in Our Time*, Workman Publishing Company, New York, 2017, p. 4.

26   Gladstone, ibid., p. 61.

27   For information on the Global Compact on Migration, go to https//
      refugeesmigrants@un.org/migration-compact.

28   See 'Major climate change report describes a strong risk of crisis as early as 2040',
      New York Times, 7 October 2018. Also, 'U.S. Government Report: Fourth National
      Climate Assessment', *New York Times*, 28 November 2018.

29   See Nicanor Perlas, *Humanity's Last Stand: The Challenge of Artificial Intelligence*,
      Temple Lodge, London, 2018, for a very interesting discussion of Artificial
      Intelligence from a spiritual perspective.

30   Parker Palmer, *Healing the Heart of Democracy: The Courage to Create a Politics
      Worthy of the Human Spirit*, Jossey-Bass, San Francisco, Calif., 2011, pp. 191–192.

31   David Hogg, Lauren Hogg, *Never Again*, Random House, New York, 2018, p. 128.

32   See Parker Palmer, p. 187.

33   Rebecca Solnit, 'Civil society at Ground Zero', in *Tom's Dispatch*, 22 November 2011.

Index

Ordering Books

If you have difficulties ordering Hawthorn Press books from a bookshop, you can order
direct from our website **www.hawthornpress.com**, or from our UK distributor
BookSource: 50 Cambuslang Road, Glasgow, G32 8NB
Tel: (0845) 370 0063, E-mail: orders@booksource.net.
Details of our overseas distributors can be found on our website.

Hawthorn Press

www.hawthornpress.com